Stealing First

and Other Old-Time Baseball Stories

CHRIS WILLIAMS

Mechanicsburg, PA USA

Published by Sunbury Press, Inc.
Mechanicsburg, Pennsylvania

www.sunburypress.com

For information about special discounts for bulk purchases, please contact Sunbury Press Orders Dept. at (855) 338-8359 or orders@sunburypress.com.

To request one of our authors for speaking engagements or book signings, please contact Sunbury Press Publicity Dept. at publicity@sunburypress.com.

FIRST SUNBURY PRESS EDITION: April 2020

Set in Adobe Garamond | Interior design by Crystal Devine | Cover by Lawrence Knorr | Edited by Lawrence Knorr.

Publisher's Cataloging-in-Publication Data
Names: Williams, Chris, author.
Title: Stealing first and other old-time baseball stories / Chris Williams.
Description: First trade paperback edition. | Mechanicsburg, PA : Sunbury Press, 2020.
Summary: Unusual baseball events and seasons are recounted spanning the 20th century.
Identifiers: ISBN 978-1-620063-83-5 (softcover).
Subjects: SPORTS & RECREATION / Baseball / History.

Product of the United States of America
0 1 1 2 3 5 8 13 21 34 55

Continue the Enlightenment!

Dedicated to my five grandsons:
Samuel, Henry, Paul, Thomas, and Benjamin

CONTENTS

—

INTRODUCTION

—

Part of the enjoyment of following Major League Baseball comes from the examination of the statistics compiled by those who play the game. In the past, this was a lot easier to do as the basic stats were relatively few and simple to follow. In the 21st century, however, the number of categories created by the sabermetrics community seems endless. Using computer research, these highly intelligent folk have aided greatly in our understanding of the game. However, the "old" way of looking at the numbers is often looked-down-upon and subtly deemed to be relatively useless. This is an opinion I do not share, and I'm certain that there many baseball fans who agree with me.

Stealing First and Other Old-Time Basebase Stories is an eclectic group of statistical historical baseball essays that utilize some of the old methods to make a point (or points). There are plenty of numbers (hopefully not too many) that I believe even the casual follower of the national past-time will be able to understand. This book is also loaded with baseball nostalgia. If you enjoy diamond history, I think you're going to like this book. I certainly hope so!

Chris Williams
March 2020

ABBREVIATIONS

AB	=	at-bats
H	=	hits
HR	=	home runs
RBI	=	runs batted-in
W	=	walks
SB	=	stolen bases
OBP	=	on base percentage
SLG	=	slugging average
2B	=	doubles
3B	=	triples
E	=	errors
PCT	=	percentage
W	=	wins
L	=	losses
ERA	=	earned run average
WHIP	=	walks and hits per innings pitched
SV	=	saves

CHAPTER 1

—

The Man Who Stole First Base

You'd have to be a real grump to not like Germany Schaefer. Even grouchy web trolls might have cracked a smile watching this guy play ball. If anyone who ever played major league baseball processed a sense of humor, it was William Herman Schaefer. Nicknamed "Germany" because of his heritage, Schaefer was quite the clown during his 15-year engagement as a player and coach. Among other antics, Schaefer attempted to steal *first base* during a game on two different occasions! I'll share more on that a little later.

The stocky infielder made his major league debut with National League's Chicago club at the tail end of the 1901 season, making just seven plate appearances. The following year, Schaefer appeared in 81 games and batted an anemic .196 in 291 at-bats. The team, then known as the Orphans, were underwhelmed by his performance and demoted him to the minors for 1903. However, before departing the Windy City, Schaefer was stationed at third base on the day in September 1902 when the famous infield combo of Tinkers, Evers, and Chance took the field together for the first time.

Schaefer toiled a couple of seasons in the minors and did well, hitting .306 and .354. The Detroit Tigers needed help in the infield and purchased him for the 1905 season. Once back in the majors, Schaefer's penchant for diamond buffoonery went full throttle.

It was raining before a game on July 4, 1906. Schaefer thought the contest should be canceled, but the umpire gave every indication that it would be played despite the soggy conditions. To make his point, Schaefer took the field wearing a raincoat and galoshes, umbrella in hand—funny stuff; I would love to see this kind of thing every-now-and-then in the 21st century. However, the umpire wasn't amused. Believing he was being mocked, he threw the madcap infielder out of the game.

Once, Schaefer strolled to the plate, wearing a monstrously big fake mustache. The umpire working the plate that day took offense and tossed the player out of the game. This ejection might seem a little heavy-handed, but there have been, and still are, folks who believe it's their responsibility to zealously guard baseball's dignity and any deviation from established norms, such as wearing fake mustaches to the plate, are simply not acceptable. This umpire was obviously one such individual; I wish that someone on-the-scene at the time would have told this fellow to relax. Baseball is a *game* after all, isn't it? Lighten-up!

Later in his career, Schaefer was a player-coach for the Senators. One afternoon, another stuffy baseball arbiter thumbed him out of the game for munching on popcorn while coaching third base! And much to the spectators' delight, on numerous occasions, Schaefer would walk the left-field foul line as if it were a tight rope in-between innings.

When asked if he thought his clowning was beneficial to his teams, the answer was in the affirmative. "It keeps our fellows in good spirits and sometimes distracts the opposing players," he explained.

Schaefer didn't limit his fooling around to the ballfield. Once, the zany player noticed umpire Jack Sheridan asleep at a table in a tavern one evening. Schaefer then proceeded to speak into the top of a drainpipe that ran down the wall next to the ump's table.

"Jack Sheridan—your time has come!" he ominously moaned.

This startled Sheridan, jarring him out of his alcohol-fueled slumber. The umpire sprung up and darted out the door. Schaefer thought this was hilarious but wasn't quite done with Sheridan. A few weeks later, Sheridan was working home plate during a game when Schaefer approached the batter's box.

"Jack Sheridan-your time has come!" the player intoned.

Instantly incensed, the umpire cursed Schaefer, calling the player a "German so-and-so!" and threw him out of the game.

Ever the comedic ham, Schaefer and Tiger teammate Charley O'Leary once performed as dancing leprechauns in a burlesque house. And on occasion, Germany did a bit of clowning on Detroit vaudeville stages.

The 175-pound Chicago, Illinois, native also liked to joke about having psychic powers and would share his predictions about the upcoming game with fans in the stands. Inserted into one game as a pinch-hitter, he even had the comical audacity to loudly announce that he was going to "hit the ball into the left-field bleachers." This was met with a combination of hoots and laughter from fans and the opposing team. This crazy prediction seemed extremely unlikely as Germany was no power hitter (he would average just one dinger per season over his long career). Any expressions of derision were quickly extinguished when Schaefer remarkably proceeded to slam the first pitch into the left-field bleachers for a game-winning home run! Not merely content to go deep after promising to do so, Schaefer proceeded to slide into each bag on his way around the bases, the whole time boisterously rattling off the play-by-play of a mock horse race in which the steed's name was Schaefer. He reportedly finished his jaunt by saying, "Ladies and Gentlemen, this concludes this afternoon's performance. I thank you for your kind attention."

And then there were the two famous steals of *first base*. In the classic baseball history, *The Glory of Their Times*, teammate Davy Jones recalled the first of these comically unusual happenings:

> . . . we had men on second and third . . . with a blood-curdling shout, he took off like a wild Indian back to first base and dove in headfirst in a cloud of dust. He figured the catcher might throw to first—since he evidently wouldn't throw to second—and then I would come home same as before. But nothing happened . . . Everybody just stood there . . . with their mouths open, not knowing what the devil was going on.
>
> The umpires were just as confused as everybody else. However, it turned out that at that time there wasn't any rule against a guy going from second back to first. So, there we were, back where we started, with Schaefer on first and me on third. And on the next pitch, darned if he didn't let out another war-whoop and take off again for second base. By this time, the Cleveland catcher evidently had enough, because he finally threw to second to get Schaefer, and when he did, I took off for home . . .

According to Jones, he and the highly unconventional Schaefer were safe on the play. Some baseball scholars doubt the veracity of the story, but Jones's account is so vivid and full-of-detail that it has the ring of truth. Two major newspapers, the *Washington Post* and the *Chicago Tribune,* have documented a day in 1911 in which Schaefer pulled the almost-exact same stunt in a game against the White Sox. Major League Baseball later instituted a rule that said a runner would be ruled out if they tried to steal a base they already had advanced from. Germany's mad dash back to the first-base bag undoubtedly helped precipitate the implementation of the new directive.

Famed sportswriter Fred Lieb once said that everybody loved, "the jovial, droll" Schaefer. Why the fellow nicknamed "Germany" was so friendly and worked so hard to make people laugh might have been rooted in a large amount of personal insecurity. Those that knew him best say that Schaefer was highly self-conscious about his face, a visage dotted with an ample supply of pockmarks. Back in the early part of the 20th century, there was little the stocky infielder could do about his facial appearance as many of today's remedies were decades away from availability. The penchant for performing and clowning around may have been an effort to divert attention away from his perceived ugliness.

Perhaps Schaefer simply loved people and thoroughly enjoyed making them laugh. What made his act so beguiling was the fact that it was good-natured and never belittling. And maybe what caused him to become baseball's first "clown prince" was a combination of this affection for his fellow man and personal insecurity. Since I'm no mental health professional, I'll limit my speculations to those two possible origins. I imagine there are plenty of other possibilities.

As a ballplayer, Schaefer was half-decent. His lifetime average of .257 is pretty good, considering he played in the Dead Ball Era. During his first full season as a member of the Tigers, 1905, the American League average was .244. Not much of a power hitter, he hit just nine home runs during his fifteen-year career. Once he did get on-base, however, Schaefer was better than most as a base stealer. He averaged 28 steals per season over the length of his career: the league average in that first full campaign was sixteen.

Schaefer was more-than-adequate with the glove. Mainly a second baseman, he did put in quite a few innings at first and third. Second was his best position; he led the AL in putouts once (1905) and then placed second in 1906. As a second sacker, he finished in the top four in double plays turned three times (1905, 1906, 1909) and in the top three in overall fielding percentage twice (1905, 1909). He was the number one guy in range factor in 1905 and 1906 and third in 1909.

So, it probably wasn't any insecurity about his status on the teams he played for that caused him to be the comic figure he was. He was a solid player who just seemed to have embedded in his DNA a strong desire and natural ability to make folks laugh.

Germany Schaefer was working as a scout for the New York Giants in May 1919 when he collapsed and died after suffering a hemorrhage related to tuberculosis. He was just 42 years old. The dreaded disease had also led to the deaths of several other players in the decade before Schaefer's untimely passing, including superstar pitcher Addie Joss. Complications from TB would later claim the life of another great hurler, Christy Mathewson, in 1925.

They may have buried the body of William Herman Schaefer in a Chicago cemetery a few days after his passing, but the man's legacy of bringing laughter and smiles to the sometimes-stuffy world of Major League Baseball is there for everyone to enjoy over a hundred years later.

Germany Schaefer loved to make people laugh during his 15-year career. (U.S. Library of Congress)

Germany Schaefer in a rare serious moment. (U.S. Library of Congress)

Umpire Jack Sheridan didn't find Schaefer amusing. (U.S. Library of Congress)

Teammate Davy Jones said he witnessed one of Schaefer's steals of first base. (U.S. Library of Congress)

Charley O'Leary. He and Schaefer occasionally performed on stage as dancing leprechauns. (U.S. Library of Congress)

CHAPTER 2

—

Lights ... Camera ... Jackie!

A lot of folks are surprised to learn that baseball great Jackie Robinson acquitted himself quite well in a one-time stint as a motion picture actor. In 1950, he starred in the autobiographical *The Jackie Robinson Story* along with Ruby Dee and Minor Watson. The film traces the early years of Jackie's life, through his multi-sport career at the University of California, military service, and his days in professional baseball.

Filmed on a tiny budget and directed by B-movie veteran Alfred E. Green, *The Jackie Robinson Story* is a lot better than might be expected. Screenwriters Arthur Mann and Lawrence Taylor came up with an earnest, compelling script that borders on sappy at times but does not cross the line. Despite a total lack of professional acting experience, Jackie Robinson does a fine job in front of the camera. Famous *New York Times* movie critic Bosley Crowther said of the ballplayers' performance:

> Robinson displayed a calm assurance and composure that
> might be envied by many a Hollywood star . . . the magnificent
> athlete conducts himself with dignity, speaks his lines well and
> clearly, and faces the camera squarely, with neither shyness nor
> conceit.

Time magazine's critic said, "The best thing about the movie is Jackie Robinson."

Robinson may not have been another Laurence Olivier, but compliments from two of the world's toughest and often-caustic film critics were high praise.

From a critical standpoint, the movie has aged well. Leonard Maltin gives *The Jackie Robinson Story* a "good" three out of a possible four-star rating. Contributors to Yahoo Movies like the flick, with an average rating of 3.5 out of 5 posted. And the Rotten Tomatoes film site calls it, "one of the best baseball biopics ever filmed."

The movie greatly benefits from the performances of Robinson's co-stars. Famous character actor Minor Watson does a superb job of channeling Dodgers› GM Branch Rickey, and the lovely Ruby Dee plays Jackie's girl (and future wife) Rae with convincing sincerity (Dee later played Robinson's mother in the 1990 docudrama, *The Court-Martial of Jackie Robinson*).

Adding zest to the production was the charismatic Louise Beavers (as Jackie's mom). Beavers, a wonderful African American actress, was long kept down by the racial attitudes prevalent in Hollywood in the 1930s and 1940s. One can imagine the poignancy Beavers must have felt being a part of this celluloid record of a major racial barrier being torn down.

The Jackie Robinson Story is available at reasonable prices. A colorized version is also available, and even a few VHS copies of this unpretentious little picture are floating around the Internet. It has shown up on cable TV a few times in recent years.

If you love baseball history, check it out to see one of the greatest ballplayers of all-time in his prime. If you're interested in the progress of race relations in America, watch it and be inspired. If you enjoy good old movies with a compelling story, *The Jackie Robinson Story* would be a great choice for a rainy Saturday afternoon along with a big bowl of popcorn. It didn't win any Academy Awards, but it's an excellent testimony to a man whose life and career marked a historical epoch.

Jackie Robinson did a fine job starring in a movie about his ground-breaking career. (1950 lobby card in the U.S. Library of Congress)

The talented Ruby Dee (middle left) played Jackie Robinson's wife in the movie. (Unknown-Eagle Lion Films)

Jackie Robinson broke baseball's color line with a vengeance, hitting .311 over a ten-year career. (Pixabay License)

Director Alfred E. Green. He knew how to make a good film on a low budget. (unknown)

CHAPTER 3

The Crisis of 1969

In 1961, two members of the New York Yankees made a historic assault on one of baseball's most cherished records. Mickey Mantle and Roger Maris slammed home runs at such a pace that both men had a legitimate shot at breaking Babe Ruth's 1927 total of 60 round-trippers. A nagging injury slowed Mantle down the stretch, and he ended up with 54 home runs. But Maris survived the relentless pressure of national media attention to finally stroke number 61 on the last day of the regular season.

Commissioner Ford Frick, a friend of Babe Ruth, decreed that since Maris had eclipsed the Bambino in 162 games instead of the 154-game schedule played in 1927, his record would be listed separately, i.e., with an asterisk. In addition, many purists were outraged, believing that hitting home runs had become too easy and that something needed to be done to cut back on "cheap" long balls.

Many in Major League Baseball's leadership were sympathetic to the concept and instructed the rules committee to devise a plan that would guarantee a return to what they considered "saner" home run totals. In 1963, the strike zone was enlarged, and home run totals did, in fact, tumble across both leagues. But, so did nearly every other offensive statistic. By 1968, the composite National League batting average had fallen to .243 (.261 in 1962). In the American League, a similar decline occurred with the composite average dropping to .230 (.255 in 1962).

In 1962, National League hitters powered 1449 home runs, but by 1968 they managed only 891 round-trippers. American League hitters did somewhat better in 1968 with 1104 homers, but that was still a steep decline from the pre-rule change total of 1552 hit in 1962. The fans weren't crazy about this unintentional return to a Dead Ball Era, and attendance at the ballparks suffered.

Worried that the growing popularity of the NFL could result in decreased revenues from things like ticket sales, television rights, and merchandising, Major League Baseball decided to take decisive action. Baseball is a big business and needs big bucks to operate. Seeing a clear downward trend in attendance since the expansion of the strike zone, leadership realized their mistake and decided to revert to the pre-1963 strike zone. Also, the rule that said the pitching mound could not be higher than ten inches would be actively enforced. At the time, several mounds were as high as fifteen inches, a height that gave pitchers a distinct advantage.

These revisions worked beautifully as batting averages, extra-base hits, and on-base percentages jumped back to levels comparable to the pre-1963 rule change. The fans approved, and attendance began to climb again.

The hitters were happy, but the pitchers were forced to adjust. And more-than-a-few experienced difficulties making the transition, including a few established hurlers. A partial list of well-known guys who saw their stats decline in 1969 includes:

- **Tommy John, Chicago White Sox**
  1968 : 10–5, 1.98 ERA, 117 K, 1.038 WHIP
  1969 : 9–11, 3.25 ERA, 128 K, 1.377 WHIP
  John's numbers in 1969 weren't bad, but they do reflect a clear drop in effectiveness. John would do OK as a starter for the next three seasons; it wasn't until he joined the Dodgers in 1972 that he would re-establish himself as one of the best left-handers in baseball.

- **Dick Farrell, Philadelphia Phillies**
  1968 : 4–6, 3.48 ERA, 57 K, 1.391 WHIP
  1969 : 3–4, 4.00 ERA, 40 K, 1.601 WHIP
  At first glance, Farrell's overall decline doesn't look very dramatic. A closer look reveals a marked increase in hits allowed per innings pitched (83 in 83 IP to 92 in 74IP), a drop in saves (12 to 3), and a sizeable decrease in strikeouts per nine innings pitched (6.2 to 4.8). For a guy who largely depended on the fastball, that last figure was a very bad sign. Farrell probably realized that he was losing what had carried him over his career and called it quits after the 1969 campaign.

- **Pat Jarvis, Atlanta Braves**
  1968 : 16–12, 2.60 ERA, 157 K, 0.984 WHIP
  1969 : 13–11, 4.43 ERA, 123 K, 1.275 WHIP
  Robert Patrick Jarvis posted a winning record in 1969, but besides that, he wasn't nearly as effective as the season before. That ERA ballooned, the WHIP jumped, and he surrendered 10 more home runs despite pitching 38.2 fewer innings. His walk total increased, too.

- **Stan Bahnsen, New York Yankees**
  1968 : 17–12, 2.05 ERA, 162 K, 1.062 WHIP
  1969 : 9–16, 3.83 ERA, 130 K, 1.414 WHIP
  It didn't take young Bahnsen long to adapt to the new circumstances; he would pitch another 13 years and enjoy a career that included win seasons of 14 (twice), 18 and 21.

- **Claude Raymond, Atlanta Braves/Montreal Expos**
  1968 : 3–5, 2.83 ERA, 37 K, 1.227 WHIP
  1969 : 3–4, 4.89 ERA, 26 K, 1.400 WHIP
  Canadian fans loved it when the Expos acquired fellow countryman Raymond in August of 1969. Unfortunately, "Frenchy" would toil for the denizens of Jarry Park through the 1971 season with mediocre results.

- **Camilo Pascual, Washington Senators**
  1968 : 13–12, 2.68 ERA, 111 K, 1.199 WHIP
  1969 : 2–5. 7.04 ERA, 37 K, 1.676 WHIP
  A solid starter for most of the 60s, Pascual enjoyed his last good season during the 1968's "Year of the Pitcher." The 1969 campaign marked the beginning of a downward spiral that would lead to his retirement after the 1971 season.

- **Woodie Fryman, Philadelphia Phillies**
  1968 : 12–14, 2.78 ERA, 151 K, 1.226 WHIP
  1969 : 12–15, 4.41 ERA, 150 K, 1.454 WHIP
  Fryman was one of the few bright spots on an aging 1968 Philly squad that finished deep in the second division. Things weren't as much fun in 1969 as his ERA, WHIP, and hits-per-inning pitched swelled to mediocre levels (243 hits over 228 innings). Undaunted, the tobacco-chewing lefty made the

needed adjustments and went on to enjoy several outstanding seasons over the balance of an 18-year career.

- **Dick Ellsworth, Boston Red Sox/Cleveland Indians**
1968 : 16–7, 3.03 ERA, 106 K, 1.189 WHIP
1969 : 6–9. 4.10 ERA, 52 K, 1.510 WHIP
A 22-game winner in 1963, Ellsworth pitched well in 1968. His effectiveness began to wane in 1969 and was out of baseball by the early seventies.

- **Al Worthington, Minnesota Twins**
1968 : 4–5, 2.71 ERA, 57 K, 1.297 WHIP
1969 : 4–1, 4.57 ERA, 51 K, 1.384 WHIP
That winning record in 1969 is largely attributable to Minnesota's formidable, division-winning offense. The poor earned run average, and so-so WHIP were two of the main reasons why Worthington's save total dropped from 18 to just three. Worthington retired after the season; he was 40, so age-related declension was probably a factor in his 1969 woes. But, had he thrived, it's not unreasonable to believe the 6'2" right-hander might have continued for at least another year or two.

- **Phil Regan, Chicago Cubs**
1968 : 10–5, 2.20 ERA, 67 K, 1.069 WHIP
1969 : 12–6, 3.70 ERA, 56 K, 1.384 WHIP
The veteran Regan's W-L was good, but like Al Worthington, he benefited from a potent attack that finished second in the league in home runs (142) and third in runs scored (720). Over the next three seasons, the man nicknamed "The Vulture" faded away with an overall record of 10–17 with just six saves.

Other major league hurlers experienced similar difficulties following the changes that favored the offense. However, others thrived even though batting averages soared, and home runs increased at a spectator-pleasing pace. Here's a partial list of some of the more successful pitchers:

■ Juan Marichal, San Francisco Giants
1968 : 26–9, 2.43 ERA, 218 K, 1.047 WHIP
1969 : 21–11, 2.10 ERA, 222 K, 0.994 WHIP
The man nicknamed "The Dominican Dandy" continued to be one of baseball's most dominant pitchers in 1969.

■ Fergie Jenkins, Chicago Cubs
1968 : 20–15, 2.63 ERA, 260 K, 1.039 WHIP
1969 : 21–15, 3.21 ERA, 284 K, 1.140 whip
1968 and 1969 were basically mirror seasons for the lanky Canadian.

■ Denny McClain, Detroit Tigers
1968 : 31–6, 1.96 ERA, 280 K, 0.905 WHIP
1969 : 24–9, 2.80 ERA, 181 K, 1.092 WHIP
McClain had a legendary season in 1968, which would have been hard for anyone to match. His 1969 numbers are very good.

■ Tom Seaver, New York Mets
1968 : 16–12, 2.20 ERA, 205 K, 0.978 WHIP
1969 : 25–7, 2,21 ERA, 208 K, 1.039 WHIP
The Mets' ace morphed into one of baseball's best in 1969.

- **Bob Gibson, St. Louis Cardinals**
  1968 : 22–9, 1.12 ERA, 268 K, 0.853 WHIP
  1969 : 20–13, 2.18 ERA, 269 K, 1.102 WHIP
  Look at that earned run average for 1968—that's not a misprint! One wonders how the right-hander lost nine games for the pennant-winning Cardinals with that ERA. Gibson continued getting them out on a regular basis in 1969.

- **Mel Stottlemyre, New York Yankees**
  1968 : 21–12, 2.45 ERA, 140 K, 1.105 WHIP
  1969 : 20–14, 2.82 ERA, 113 strikeouts, 1.201 WHIP
  The righty from Hazelton, Missouri, posted his third twenty-win season in 1969 with most of his numbers like those he put up in 1968.

- **Steve Carlton, St. Louis Cardinals**
  1968 : 13–11, 2.99 ERA, 162 K, 1.185 WHIP
  1969 : 17–11, 2.17 ERA, 210 K, 1.176 WHIP
  Young "Lefty" Carlton was in the early stages of his Hall-of-Fame career when Major League Baseball reduced the size of the strike zone. Intelligent and disciplined, Carlton flourished in 1969.

- **Phil Niekro, Atlanta Braves**
  1968 : 14–12, 2.59 ERA, 140 K, 1.064 WHIP
  1969 23–13, 2.56 ERA, 193 K, 1.027 WHIP
  One of the best pitchers to never win the Cy Young Award, what makes the knuckleballer's stats in 1969 impressive is the fact that not only did he need to adjust to the new strike zone and lower mound, he made half of his starts in one of the best hitter's parks in baseball history, Atlanta Stadium.

- Eddie Watt, Baltimore Orioles
  1968 : 5–5, 2.27 ERA, 72 K, 1.176 WHIP
  1969 : 5–2, 1.65 ERA, 46 K, 1.056 WHIP
  What rule changes? The guy signed as an amateur free agent in
  1961 went from very good in 1968 to excellent in 1969.

- Larry Dierker, Houston Astros
  1968 : 12–15, 3.31 ERA, 161 K, 1.262 WHIP
  1969 : 20–13, 2.33 ERA, 232 K, 1.022 WHIP
  The 22-year-old fireballer prospered despite the shrunken
  strike zone and lower mound. Although 1969 was the only
  season in which he would win 20 games, Dierker finished his
  14-year career with a good .533 lifetime winning percentage
  despite pitching for several unexceptional/or lousy Astro teams.

It's open to debate how much the smaller strike zone and lower
mound might have affected the performance of each pitcher men-
tioned here. In cases involving guys in their mid-to-late 1930s, a
normal, age-related decline might have been a factor. But it's also
possible that those same players had greatly benefited from the
expanded strike zones and mountainous pitching mounds in the
preceding years. The same could be said about the younger hurlers who fell-off statistically in 1969. *It's a fact that offensive totals in
both leagues jumped significantly immediately after the rule changes.*
It seems logical to assume that these modifications contributed to
higher batting averages, more home runs, and increased runs scored.
Subsequently, any pitcher who fared poorly after good seasons in
1968 very well may have been hurt by baseball's new paradigm.

The "survivors" who continued to succeed in 1969 included
some of the greatest names in baseball history. Perhaps, it was partially happenchance, but more likely, their triumphs were due in
large part to some having more natural ability than many of their

contemporaries, who struggled, talent that compensated well for the loss of advantage. The smarter guys, not just the elite, were able to figure out what needed to be done to continue to perform at a high level. Others couldn't (or wouldn't) make the needed adjustments in their mechanics and mental approach.

The competitors who successfully adapted were often younger players. The ten hurlers discussed in this article averaged 26.6 years of age in 1969, while the pitchers who scuffled averaged 31.8-years-old. Older people, in general, not just baseball players, are often resistant to change and tend to be creatures of habit. Reluctant to vary what worked well for them in the past, some of the elder pitchers may have stuck with the familiar and paid for it with mediocre or poor statistics. Youth are usually more open to new thought, and many of those who succeeded in 1969 might have willingly embraced the smaller strike zone and lower mound as stimulating challenges or, at the very least, viewed them as manageable problems.

A balance of sorts returned to baseball in 1969. There were still great pitchers who compiled impressive stats, but the number of position players with notable offensive accomplishments jumped, too. Sabermatician-extraordinaire Bill James thinks the type of baseball played over the next decade was "wonderful." He says:

> On the field, at one time you might have a player who was capable of hitting .350 or better, a baserunner who was capable of stealing 80 or more bases, a hitter who was capable of hitting 35 or 40 homers, and a 20-game winner who could strike out 250–300 batters. —*The New Bill James Historical Baseball Abstract*, pg. 277

The fans loved it. Overall attendance spiked from a little over 224 million during the 1960s to almost 331 million in the 1970s.

Baseball's "bean counters" were quite happy, too. The revenue stream would continue undiminished and increase over the next several decades, thanks to increased turnout at the ballparks, lucrative TV and radio deals, and highly profitable merchandising agreements. By the 21st century, the crisis of 1969 was a distant memory.

However, at the time, it threatened the careers and livelihood of many players and the long-term financial viability of Major League Baseball.

One-time-ace Camilio Pascual's ERA
ballooned from 2.68 in 1968 to 7.04 in 1969.
(*Baseball Guide and Record Book* 1962)

1969 was the end-of-the line for Phillies reliever Dick Farrell.
(Manny's Baseball Land via tradingcarddb.com)

Smaller strike zone? No Problem! Juan Marichal of the Giants lowered his ERA and WHIP in 1969. (Jay Publishing via tradingcarddb.com)

Young Steve Carlton blossomed in 1969 to become one of baseball's best pitchers. (St. Louis Cardinals via tradingcarddb.com)

When Roger Maris (#9 above) slammed a then-record of 61 longballs in 1961, some believed that home runs had become a little too easy to hit. (Detroit Free Press Archives)

1969 saw the beginning of a
four-year slide in effectiveness
for one-time stand-out reliever
Phil Regan.
(By Unknown - Jewel Tea via
tradingcarddb.com)

Major League Baseball in the 1980s was an exciting, fast-paced game. The fans loved it.
(Creative Commons CC0 1.0 Universal Public Domain Dedication)

CHAPTER 4

The Great Collapse of 1964 Revisited

Much has been written about the epic collapse of the 1964 Phillies. With 12 games to play, the club had a 6½ game lead and looked destined to appear in their first World Series in 14 years. What happened is still hard for many old-time Philly fans to believe; the team lost 10-games straight, and the red-hot Cardinals raced by them to win the National League flag by one game.

Over the ensuing years, many explanations have been offered for the Phillies' infamous late-season swoon. Many point to the early September injury that knocked Frank Thomas out of action as being a major cause of the team's downfall. First base had been a weak spot in the club's line-up, and the mid-season acquisition of Thomas had given the team quite a boost (.294 AVG, 7 HRs in 39 games). Besides, injuries to pitchers Dennis Bennett and Art Mahaffey hurt the club at a time when they should have been "closing the deal" and getting ready to play in the Fall Classic. Manager

Gene Mauch responded by using his aces, Jim Bunning and Chris Short, several times on just a couple of days rest. The Phils' skipper planned to give the pair ample rest once the pennant had been secured. The results were catastrophic as both men were unable to perform at the high level they had achieved before the collapse.

It was this mishandling of the pitching staff that is often cited as the main reason why the 1964 Phillies tanked it. But in retrospect, a look at the teams involved in the great drama of the 1964 pennant race indicated a more likely reason why the Phils were unable to hold-on.

The Phils had a fine team that year. But were they as good as the St. Louis Cardinals? Let's compare some of the stats for 1964:

- **Catcher**
  (PHIL) Dalrymple – .238 AVG, .303 OBP, 6 HRs
  (STL) McCarver – .288 AVG, .343 OBP, 9 HRs
  Edge: Cardinals. Dalrymple was better defensively, but McCarver was no slouch behind-the-plate and was a much better hitter.

- **First Base**
  (PHIL) Herrnstein – .234 AVG, .288 OBP, 6 HRs.
  (PHIL) Thomas – .294 AVG, .311 OBP, 7 HRs.
  (STL) White – .303 avg, .355 OBP, 21 HRs, 102 RBIs
  Edge: Cardinals. Bill White was one of the finest first sackers in MLB in the 1960s. His 1964 output was a typical season for him. Not only could he hit, but he also won 13 Gold Gloves during his career. Frank Thomas was a slow-footed, average fielder who could hit for some power. Who'd you rather have? And John Herrnstein? Pleeeeeease . . .

■ **Second Base**

(PHIL) Taylor – .251 AVG, .320 OBP, 13 SB

(STL) Javier – .241 avg, .282 OBP

Edge: Slightly to the Phillies. Both season and career-wise, Taylor was a better player. However, Javier was an infield anchor on three Cardinal pennant winners and was named to two All-Star teams. If his career OBP had been a little higher, the edge might have gone to St. Louis.

■ **Shortstop**

(PHIL) Wine – .212 AVG, .274 OBP

(PHIL) Amaro – .264 AVG, .307 OBP

(STL) Groat – .292 AVG, .335 OBP, 70 RBIs

Edge: Both Wine and Amaro were superb fielders, but career-wise they were offensive lightweights (although Amaro did have a respectable average in 1964 and drove in many key runs). Groat made the plays he needed to make in the field and was exponentially better at the plate than Wine and Amaro combined. A positional victory for the Cardinals.

■ **Third Base**

(PHIL) Allen – .318 AVG, .382 OBP, 29 HRs, 91 RBIs

(STL) Boyer – .295 AVG, .365 OBP, 24 HRs, 119 RBIs

Edge: Phillies. "Rookie of the Year" Allen gets the edge over Ken Boyer at third base but not by much. Allen did hit for a higher average and slugged more homers, but Boyer drove-in 28 more runs. Also, Allen led the league in errors with 40 while Boyer was a 5-time Gold Glove winner. For his efforts, Boyer was named National League MVP at the end of the season.

I think Allen rates slightly higher because of the players that surrounded him in the line-up. Boyer played alongside a virtual All-Star team; pitching around him was risky business, Allen didn't have the protection around him in the line-up that Boyer had in St. Louis. It had to be harder for the man from Wampum, Pennsylvania, to compile his impressive numbers in 1964.

- Outfield
(PHIL) Covington – .280 AVG, .355 OBP, 13 HRs, 58 RBI
(PHIL) Gonzalez – .278 AVG, .352 OBP
(PHIL) Callison – .274 AVG, .316 OBP, 31 HRs, 104 RBI
(STL) Flood – .311 AVG, .356 OBP, 211 hits
(STL) Brock – .348 AVG, .387 OBP, 12 HRs, 33 SB
(STL) Shannon – .261 AVG, .310 OBP, 9 HRs
Edge: Cardinals. Johnny Callison's power numbers were good but his on-base-percentage was so-so. Patrolling the outfield with him were veterans Tony Gonzalez and Wes Covington, both decent players who could hit a little. Neither were exactly perennial all-stars. In the Cardinal outfield, you had All-Star gold-glover Curt Flood, future All-Star and base stealing champion Lou Brock, and Mike Shannon who drilled nine homeruns in 253 at-bats.

    Defensively, the Phillies compare well in the outfield. Flood was the best-of-them-all, but Callison was very good and had a rifle arm. Gonzalez was an excellent fielder, but Covington was mediocre. Brock was better than Covington, but he wasn't great, even in his prime. Shannon didn't embarrass himself with the glove, but Gonzalez was much better at running down those fly balls.

    Close, but St. Louis wins this match-up.

- Bench
Edge: Phillies. This one isn't even close. Cookie Rojas, one-of-the-premier utility men of the era, posted the second highest batting average of his career in 1964 (.291) Danny Cater hit

close to .300 before going down with an injury, and Alex Johnson gave a glimpse of the offensive powerhouse he would later become by hitting .303 in a part-time role. A young Johnny Briggs gave the club some left-handed power off the bench, and the man who caught Jim Bunning's perfect game, Gus Triandos, smacked in 8 home runs in limited playing time.

Rojas was a good fielder, at his best playing middle infield, and except for Johnson, the others were adequate defensively. As bad as Johnson was with the glove, at least he looked like he was trying most-of-the-time.

The Cardinals bench was OK, but except for Bob Skinner (.333 OBP), none of the subs seemed to know the value of taking a pitch and working a walk. Charlie James (5 HRs, 17 RBIs) supplied some pop, and Bob Uecker was a good defensive catcher. But Philly's bench was better.

■ **Starting Pitching**
(PHIL) Bunning – 19–8, 2.63 ERA, 1.03 WHIP, 219 K
(PHIL) Short – 17–9, 2.20 ERA, 1.02 WHIP, 181 K
(PHIL) Bennett – 12–14, 3.68 ERA, 222 hits allowed in 208 innings, 23 HRs
(PHIL) Mahaffey – 12–9, 4.52 ERA, 17 HRs allowed in 157innings
(PHIL) Culp – 8–7, 4.13 ERA, 15 HRs allowed in 135 innings
(STL) Gibson – 19–12, 3.01 ERA, 1.16 WHIP, 245 K
(STL) Simmons – 18–9, 3.43 ERA, 1.15 WHIP
(STL) Sadecki – 20–11, 3.68 ERA
(STL) Craig – 7–9, 3.25 ERA
Edge: Bunning and Short were outstanding in 1964 and compiled better stats than the front two in the Cardinal rotation (Gibson and Simmons). But Bob and Curt were pretty darn good, and Sadecki and Craig were better than the combination

of Bennett, Mahaffey and Culp. Philly starters 3. 4 and 5 were virtual homerun machines; Bunning let up a lot of long balls too but that was true throughout his long career. His propensity for serving-up the gopher was balanced by low hits allowed totals, great walk ratios, and tons of strikeouts. Bennet, Mahaffey and Culp just served up a lot of homeruns in 1964 while allowing too many hits and walks.

Even Ernie Broglio posted better numbers (3.50 ERA, 61 hits allowed in 69 innings) before being traded to the Cubs than either Bennett, Mahaffey, or Culp.

In Bennett's defense, he did "soldier on" in September with a sore arm, which limited his effectiveness.

Edge: St. Louis wins this one. Most managers would love to start a season with a rotation as good as the 1964 Cardinals.

■ Bullpen

Edge: Cardinals. Barney Shultz may have been the best reliever in the NL in 1964 (22 saves, 1.64 ERA). His one home run allowed is even more impressive when you consider the fact that St. Louis played their home games in old Busch Stadium, a hitter-friendly venue. Philly closer Jack Baldschun was OK in 1964, but with a 3.12 ERA and 1.28 WHIP, it wasn't exactly "lights-out" for the opposition.

Ed Roebuck pitched well for the Phillies (2.21 ERA, 12 saves), but after that, mediocrity. Rookie Rick Wise showed promise, but John Boozer and Dallas Green were absolutely no help. The front three in the Cardinals pen averaged allowing under three-runs-per game and the back-end guys, although not spectacular, were much better than Philly's dispensers of gasoline.

The Phillies fare well when both teams' overall performance is considered:

- The Cardinals had the highest team batting average in the NL (.272). The Phillies finished fourth at .258.
- The Cardinals finished second in the league in triples, second in OBP and second in total bases. The Phils finished third in triples, third in OBP and fifth in total bases. Philadelphia did hit one more double than St. Louis (241–240).
- The Phillies slugged more homers (130–109).
- The Phillies were slightly better in the field (.975) than the Cards (.973).
- The Cardinals registered 43 complete games by their pitchers as opposed to 37 for Philly.
- The Phillies overall staff era was 3.36 compared to 3.43 for the Cards. (However, the overall era for the top five players used in each team's bullpen isn't even close. For St. Louis, the figure is 2.96. For Philadelphia, 4.51).

As you can see, even in the handful of statistical areas that St. Louis ranked behind Philadelphia, they weren't *that* far behind.

After examining the statistics, I believe the better team ended up winning the 1964 National League pennant. Rather than blame Gene Mauch, or injuries, or the fates, it might be more truthful to face reality.

For 150 games, the Phillies far-exceeded what could have been reasonably-expected of the talent on their roster. Some-sort-of correction may have been inevitable.

A historic collapse?

Perhaps not.

Sometimes, good teams do find a way to nudge ahead of better clubs and make it to the post-season.

And that's what *almost* happened in 1964.

It isn't fair to completely blame skipper Gene Mauch for Philly's 1964 collapse. (Manny's Baseball Land via tradingcarddb.com)

Fireballer Bob Gibson won 19 games to help the Cardinals capture the 1964 National League pennant. (Baseball Digest 1962)

The acquisition of righty Jim Bunning from the Tigers helped make the 1964 Phillies pennant contenders. (JG Howes from the 1957 Detroit Tigers Official Profile, Photo and Data Book.)

Speedster Lou Brock batted a sizzling .348 for the Cardinals after being acquired in a trade with the Cubs in June. (Jay Publishing via tradingcarddb.com)

Two-time All-Star catcher Tim McCarver. (St. Louis Cardinals via tradingcarddb.com)

Cardinals third baseman Ken Boyer was the NL MVP in 1964. (St. Louis Cardinals via tradingcarddb.com)

Left-hander Chris Short won 17 games and posted a low 2.20 ERA for the 1964 Phils. (Sports Service via tradingcarddb.com)

CHAPTER 5

A Headache Had Nothing to Do with It

Wally Pipp deserves a little bit of posthumous respect. He certainly had a lot of it around the American League the day a hulking Columbia graduate was awarded the position Pipp had held down for the previous ten seasons. For several years, the guy Lou Gehrig replaced as the starting first baseman for the New York Yankees was one of the best players in baseball.

When skipper Miller Huggins inserted Gehrig into the line-up in June of 1925, nobody could have imagined that the man was destined to play in the next 2,129 Yankee games. (The Iron Horse's record of 2,130 consecutive games began the day before as a pinch-hitter.) Pipp didn't just fade away after that fateful day; the veteran first sacker put in four more productive seasons with a couple of other teams before retiring after the 1929 campaign.

Walter Clement Pipp began his major league baseball career in 1913 as a member of the Detroit Tigers. A 0 for 3 performance in his first game was a harbinger of the only season he would spend as a player in the Motor City. Used sparingly, Pipp managed a minuscule .161 batting average that included just three extra-base hits. The Tigers were less-than-impressed and sent the young first baseman down to the Providence Grays, an AA team in the International League.

Pipp blossomed in 1914, hitting .314 and leading the International League in home runs with 15. He also stroked 27 triples and compiled an impressive .526 slugging percentage.

The upstart Federal League had begun operations as a major league in 1914. Seeking to gain a foothold in America's largest market, they placed a team in Brooklyn, New York. Also, the new league announced plans to move their Indianapolis franchise to nearby Newark, New Jersey, for the 1915 season. These two new clubs would provide direct competition for fan support for the established Dodgers and Yankees. To strengthen the Yankees, who had been floundering over the previous decade, the Detroit Tigers sold Pipp and another player to them for a total of 10,000 dollars.

Pipp's first season in Yankee pinstripes was half-decent. He only hit .246 but did smash 13 triples and registered a respectable .339 OBP. His league-leading .992 fielding percentage also saved a few runs for the pitching staff. The young man from Chicago, Illinois, was maturing, quickly learning the major league game, and growing more confident each day.

Beginning with the 1916 season, Wally Pipp became an offensive force to be reckoned with. He hit 12 home runs to lead the American League, drove-in 92 runs to place second overall, and legged-out the league's fifth-highest number of triples (14). The next season, Pipp once again led the league in homers (9) and finished in the top ten in triples, doubles, runs scored, total bases, and RBI.

(The home run totals might seem low to the modern reader but keep in mind, Pipp's numbers were compiled during a time when the ball used wasn't as lively as it is now, the dimensions of many of the ballparks were much larger, and pitchers were allowed to throw now-illegal pitches like the spit and emery "shine" balls.)

Wally continued his steady glove work in 1916 and 1917, finishing third among AL first baseman both seasons with stellar fielding averages of .992 and .990.

For the next several seasons, the lefty slugger kept getting better. From 1918 through 1925, Pipp's batting averages ranged from .275 to .329. And although he never led the league in home runs again, he did finish in the top ten for long balls hit three times, drove in over 100 runs thrice and 94 once, and led the league in triples once.

Pipp also continued being a dandy at the first base bag during this period. Quick-as-a-cat, he was the top guy in the American League five times in turning the double play. Once, he led his first base peers in fielding percentage, once placed second, and four times finished in the top three.

The *New York Times* said the first baseman at this time was "a high-class specimen of the ballplayer."

And indeed, he was. Wally Pipp might have the biggest star on the Yankees when Babe Ruth joined the team in 1920. Ruth quickly became not only the Bronx Bombers' biggest star, but his prodigious hitting also made him one of the most famous people in the world. In his first season with New York, Ruth batted an incredible .376, pounded a then-record 54 home runs, and plated 135 of his teammates. A new, tighter-center ball had been introduced that year, a spheroid that did travel farther when solid contact was made. But no other *team* in the American League hit more than 50 round-trippers for the season. What the flamboyant Ruth accomplished in 1920 and during many seasons that followed was nothing short of incredible.

There's no indication that Pipp resented the Babe's ascendency as the team's number one guy. If he did, it didn't last long as the Yankees improved by 15 games in 1920 and began to win pennants in '21. Fans were going through the turnstiles like-never-before, putting more cash into Yankee coffers. This resulted in more money available for player salaries. By 1923, Pipp's baseball wages had jumped from 5,000 to 10,000 dollars-a-year.

Pipp and Ruth became friends and drinking buddies. Pipp's daughter Mary marveled at how much alcohol the pair could consume. She said the pair "could consume a fifth of vodka and have a big game the next day." But when Ruth criticized Pipp for making a costly error during a game in 1922, Pipp took exception, and a fight ensued. Several teammates were needed to separate the combatants. However, the two reconciled and continued to be friends. Years later, Pipp said he believed the altercation had a positive effect on a Yankee team that had been struggling:

"That fight cleared the atmosphere a lot. We stopped stumbling and fumbling as a club and went on to win the pennant."

The hard-hitting first baseman was a bit of an iron man himself. From 1915 to 1924, Pipp played in no fewer than 136 games each season, save for one year, and in over 150 six times (an injury limited him to 91 games in 1918). Pipp managed to stay in the Yankee line-up even though he suffered from periodic, chronic headaches, the result of being hit in the head with a hockey puck as a youth.

Pipp told an interviewer in 1953 that it was a headache that forced him out of the line-up on that fateful day when Lou Gehrig replaced him at first base. But it wasn't one of his "usual" headaches; this one he said was caused by a beaning in batting practice the day before on June 1. Pipp added that the injury forced him to spend the following two weeks in the hospital.

The old ball player's recollection wasn't quite accurate. According to records, Pipp pinch-hit for Gehrig on June 3 and then entered the game as a defensive replacement in a 6–4 Yankee win over the Senators. Pipp did suffer a batting practice beaning, but it occurred on July 2 of that year, resulting in a fractured skull or concussion. The one-time starting first baseman did spend some time in the hospital following the beaning; when he was cleared to play again, the Yankees used him sparingly.

What many baseball historians believe is that skipper Miller Huggins replaced a slumping Pipp (who was only hitting .244 at the time) with Gehrig to revitalize an underachieving Yankee squad. At that point in the season, the Bronx Bombers were scuffling with a poor record of 15–26 and had dropped five-straight. Huggins benched several veterans in hopes of rekindling a Yankee attack that had captured three pennants over the previous four years. These efforts failed as the Yankees plummeted all the way to seventh place with a 69–85 record.

When weighing the documented evidence (or lack thereof), the belief that Pipp asked to be taken out of the lineup because of a headache is a myth. This piece of false baseball lore was almost assuredly abetted by Pipp's own inaccurate account of the events that surrounded Gehrig's insertion as New York's starting first baseman. Plus, the established fact that Pipp did suffer from chronic headaches added validity to the untrue narrative that he lost his job because he was a malingerer who was just looking for a day off.

In a little more-than-half-a-season, Gehrig finished 1925 with 20 home runs, 68 RBIs, and a .295 average. The Yankees had a productive new first baseman, one that was ten years younger than the fellow who previously filled the position. Wally Pipp, who ended the season with a .230 average, was purchased by the Cincinnati

Reds in the off-season. Was he bitter about his banishment from Yankee pinstripes?

"Huggins would have been a complete dope to give my job back," Pipp said in his later years.

The 6'1", 180-pounder was solid in his first season in Cincy. A healthy Pipp played in 155 games, hit .291, and knocked-in 99 runs. As-sure-handed with the glove as ever, he placed second overall among National League first sackers in fielding percentage (.992).

In 1927, he ranked first in fielding (.996), but his batting average dipped to .260. A future Hall-of-Famer by the name of George "High Pockets" Kelly outplayed him in 1928 to earn the Reds' starting first base job. Pipp performed well as a part-timer, batting .283 with a respectable .341 OBP in 95 games.

After the 1928 campaign, Pipp and the Reds parted ways. The former Catholic University of America student wrapped-up his baseball career at the age of 36 as a member of the minor league Newark Bears in 1929. Pipp went out in style, hitting .312 for the International League club while smashing 30 doubles and 12 home runs.

Wally Pipp experienced an active and eventful life after hanging up his spikes. A heavy investor in the Stock Market, he was nearly wiped out financially in the 1929 crash. He owed a lot of people a ton of money and nearly needed to declare bankruptcy but eventually managed to pay off his creditors.

For several years he hosted a pre-game radio show for the Detroit Tigers. Pipp also wrote a cautionary book about his bad experiences in the stock market and was involved in starting baseball programs for young people across the country. During World War II, the man who finished with a .281 lifetime major league average worked at a factory building bomber planes. Later, he made a living selling machine parts to various industries.

Pipp was residing in a Michigan nursing home when a series of strokes claimed his life in 1965. The former star first baseman was 71.

It's a shame that Pipp is mainly remembered today as the man Lou Gehrig replaced at first base. It's unfair that his legacy has been tarnished by the fairy tale that he used a headache as an excuse to ask his manager for a day off. The idea that he wanted a day to chill on the bench doesn't seem logical. Mr. Pipp, who suffered from headaches all his adult life, must have performed though more-than-a-few of them over the previous ten seasons, nine of which he was in the line-up practically every day.

Being replaced by a great player like Lou Gehrig was no dishonor. Pipp was very good but never put up the type of incredible numbers "Laruppin' Lou" did during his illustrious 17-year-career. However, how many players (not just first basemen) over the years have? Precious few.

Gehrig's predecessor ought to be mainly remembered for *his* many on-the-field accomplishments in Yankee pinstripes.

The fact is Wally Pipp was one heckuva player.

The man who replaced two-time American League home run champ Wally Pipp as Yankees first baseman. What was his name again? (U.S. Library of Congress)

Although he was no Lou Gehrig, Wally Pipp was a darn good player himself. (U.S. Library of Congress)

Yankees manager Miller Huggins. The man he inserted into the lineup for star Wally Pipp become one of the greatest players of all-time. (US Library of Congress)

The great Babe Ruth touching the plate after another home run. He and Wally Pipp were drinking buddies. (Paul Thompson 1878–1940)

Panic gripped Wall Street in October 1929. The crash nearly bankrupted Pipp.
(From an SSA poster: http://www.ssa.gov/history/wallst.html)

—

CHAPTER 6

—

What a Difference a Hundred Years Makes

The year 1901 was a long time ago.

A *long* time ago.

America has changed in innumerable ways since the earliest days of the 20th century. Transportation, once slow and generally devoid of creature comforts, now enables travelers to go to destinations near and far much faster and in relative comfort. Advancements in medicine, food safety, hygiene practices, and sanitation have lifted the life expectancy in the U.S. from 49.1 years in 1901 to 78.9 years in 2016. The media has exploded with a breath-taking proliferation of print, electronic and digital media over the decades that would have astounded Americans at the turn of the 20th century. Many other instances of profound change could be cited; suffice to say that the USA in 1901 was a much different place than it is in the 21st century.

Like the rest of society, Major League Baseball looked different in 2001 when compared to a hundred years earlier. The American League (AL) debuted in 1901, with eight teams playing a 136-game schedule. The National League (NL), around since 1876, also had eight teams but played a 140-game schedule. In 2001, the AL featured 14 teams, and the NL fielded 16 clubs with both leagues using a 162-game schedule.

Strategies were different in the early part of the 20th century. For example, let's look at the pennant winners for both seasons. In 1901, home runs were few and far between, so managers needed to rely more on speed and strategy to generate runs. The home run leader on the AL pennant-winning Chicago White Sox was second baseman Sam Mertes who hit just five all season long. The NL champion Pittsburgh Pirates' dinger leader was an outfielder by the name of Ginger Beaumont, who slugged eight round-trippers.

A hundred years later, first baseman Tino Martinez led the AL pennant-winning New York Yankees with 34 home runs. Over in the NL, outfielder Luis Gonzalez led the champion Arizona Diamondbacks with 57 fence-clearing bombs (the league leader that year hit 73 home runs!) As teams, the Yankees and Diamondbacks smacked a lot more home runs (203, 208) than the 1901 White Sox and Pirates (32, 29).

What caused the difference in the number of long balls? For starters, the ball used in the 21st century is made of higher-quality material and travels farther when solid contact is made. Also, many modern-day players work on physical conditioning year-round, including muscle-building weightlifting. They are paid much better than their counterparts in 1901, don't need to worry as much about paying the bills, and have a lot-more-free time for conditioning. Nearly all the old-time players *needed* to work another job in the off-season to take care of themselves and their families. Many would use Spring Training to get into shape for the regular season. Most of today's ballplayers show-up to training camp in February in good physical condition.

In other words, a livelier ball and stronger players with the ability to power those balls over the fence has led to a major increase in the number of home runs hit.

Another important difference is the number of baseballs used during a game has grown considerably over the decades. In 1901, balls were kept in play for as long as possible, and by the late innings were often dark and dirty and harder to see. In 2001, hitters were treated to nice clean balls to see in almost every at-bat. This difference obviously benefits the hitter and helps increase those home run totals.

An additional advantage to the modern baseball player is the prohibition against illegal pitches that helped pitchers throw balls that spun, curved, and jumped in hard-to-hit ways. The most famous of these pitches is known as the "Spitball"; pitchers would use saliva, petroleum jelly, and some other substance to make the ball do unexpected things on the way to home plate. Pitchers in 2001 (and today) aren't allowed to use these pitches, but back in 1901, they weren't illegal. There were more-than-a-few hurlers who occasionally (or often) "doctored" the ball with various substances at the turn-of-the-century.

Despite the disadvantages, some players compiled impressive stats that compare quite well when compared to 2001 and, in some cases, even better. For example, Honus Wagner's .353 average in 1901 was tops on the NL champion Pirates. The top batting average on the 2001 NL Champs, the Diamondbacks, was registered by Luis Gonzalez, who hit .325.

The next two highest averages by regulars on the Pirates were .332 and .324; on the Diamondbacks, the next highest were .298 and .275.

Stolen base totals in 1901 far exceeded those of 2001. The pennant-winning White Sox and Pirates stole a total of 503 bases between them. One hundred years later, the two teams that won their leagues managed to swipe a total of 201 bases, about 40 percent of the 1901 totals. The players at the turn-of-the-century weren't necessarily faster or smarter than those of 2001; most teams in the 21st century don't *need* to steal a lot of bases to put runs on the board.

The number of triples hit in 1901 was considerably higher as players were more willing to take a chance at that extra base rather than wait for a teammate to jerk one out of the park. In 2001, playing an average of 24 more games-per-season than a hundred years earlier, the 18 teams in the big leagues stroked a total of 928 triples. In 1901, a total of 1238 three-baggers were hit over that full season.

If the ball was so "dead," why the high number of triples?

There are two important reasons:

• Necessity. Teams needed to do a lot of running to score enough runs to win. Playing it safe didn't cut it; they had to make things *happen*. In the 21st century, you might look like a chump if you get thrown out at third and the guy batting after you hits a 415-foot home run.

• Dimensions at the old-time ballparks were a factor in the scarcity of home runs but aided in the proliferation of three-baggers. It was a long way to most of the fences back then, as much as 500 to 600 feet in some cases. While outfielders chased balls hit in the gap or over their heads, hitters had time to turn what would have been a double in 2001 into a triple.

Statistics for pitchers in the early years of the 20th century are, at least on the surface, much better than those compiled today. For instance, compare some overall important numbers for the pennant-winning staffs of 1901 and 2001:

1901 Pittsburgh Pirates
2.58 ERA, 1.159 WHIP, 15 SHO, 119 complete games

2001 Arizona Diamondbacks
3.87 ERA, 1.242 WHIP, 13 SHO, 12 complete games

1901 Chicago White Sox
2.98 ERA, 1.282 WHIP, 11 SHO, 131 complete games

2001 New York Yankees
4.02 ERA, 1.305 WHIP, 3 SHO, 7 complete games

To the casual observer, the pitchers on the 1901 league champs were much better than those who toiled in 2001. The Diamondbacks came close to matching the White Sox and Pirates in the number of shutouts, but they and the Yankees didn't come close in the other categories. The overall league earned run average for the two leagues in 2001 was also much higher, too (4.41 to 3.49). And look at those complete games! In 1901, major league hurlers logged 2220 complete games; a hundred years later, the big leagues witnessed the starter going the distance 199 times.

Were pitchers in the first year of the AL/NL set-up superior to those laboring on the mound in the second year of the 21st century?

No, not really.

All the conditions that stifled offensive production contributed to the success of many pitchers in 1901. A less-than-lively ball that was often hard to see, doctored pitches, and faraway ballpark fences helped keep those earned run averages low. The big difference in complete games could be explained by the fact that pitchers were counted on to go the full nine innings and were usually only taken out of a game if they were getting bombed or seriously injured.

Hurlers were expected to work through things like tiredness and minor aches and pains. In 2001 (and today), the starting pitcher isn't expected to go "the full nine" for their team. If he does, great. Ball clubs have relief specialists who can enter a game when the starter begins to falter. The 21st-century mindset is that a fresh arm is more likely to get batters out in key situations than a tired one. In 1901, that was not the plan.

Batters in the early part of the 20th century were aided by the size of the gloves worn by fielders. Mitts were small and crude when compared to the much larger and well-made ones used in the 21st century. Many balls that would have eluded a fielder in 1901 are now being snared by players using gloves with big webbing. Although the use of smaller gloves helped hitters at the turn of the century, it didn't help nearly enough to offset the advantages enjoyed by pitchers.

The method that teams used to travel was vastly different. At the turn of the century, the train was the mode of transportation for distant road trips. These journeys by rail were often long, hot, uncomfortable, and sometimes even dangerous. Hot coal ashes from steam engines would occasionally float through an open window or screen to burn a player's skin or clothing. Players often arrived at their destination tired from a less-than-comfortable trip and not at their best mentally and physically. In the 21st century, ball clubs hop aboard luxurious jet planes to arrive at far-away places. For closer destinations, modern teams sometimes use air-conditioned buses with padded seats to get where they want to go. This ease of transport enables ballplayers to arrive more energetic and ready to play than their 1901 counterparts.

Attendance at major league baseball games is another difference between the 1901 and 2001 seasons. An average of 3,599 fans attended a NL champion Pirates home game in 1901; for the AL winning White Sox, the average was higher at 5,211. Move ahead to 2001, and the number of people attending games skyrockets; the Yankees played before an average home crowd of 40,307, and the World Champion Diamondbacks averaged 33,783 patrons per home contest.

There are others, but some of the reasons for the massive increase in attendance include:

- The population of the United States in 1901 was just over 77.5 million people; by 2001, it had swelled to almost 285 million. More people created the possibility of more interest in professional baseball and higher attendance figures at ball games.
- The coverage of big-league baseball in 1901 was limited to the print media, mainly newspapers. There were far fewer opportunities to publicize and promote the sport. By the 21st century, baseball was receiving nearly 24-hour media saturation coverage via TV, radio, print, and the Internet. Baseball can reach significantly more people, which has resulted in substantially more fan support.
- With technological breakthroughs making work easier and less time-consuming, people have more hours for leisure activities in the 21st century. Attending major league baseball games is one way a lot of people have decided to fill that time and spend some of their income.
- Improved modes of transportation, the automobile-in-particular. Ownership of cars has allowed Americans to safely travel, sometimes far distances, to stadiums in comfort. Few people had cars in 1901, and the ones that were on the road were rudimentary and not built to travel great distances.

Another major difference between the 1901 and 2001 seasons is the fact that no World Series was played following the regular season. In the beginning, the two leagues were fierce competitors, with the AL luring many NL players away from their teams with bigger contracts. The older league fiercely resisted this at first, but eventually, the two sides came to an agreement, the terms of which included a post-season match-up between the teams with the best record in each league. In 1903, the Boston Americans of the AL beat the NL Pittsburgh Pirates five games to three in what is considered the first World Series.

In 1904, the New York Giants refused to play Boston in a post-season match-up of league champions because the New Yorkers believed they didn't need to prove how much better they thought they were than the upstarts in Beantown. Giants Manager John McGraw let it be known that he was certain that his team was vastly superior to *any* club in the American League. In response, baseball leadership mandated that the two league winners would meet each year after the regular season to decide an overall champion. Individual clubs no longer had the right to simply refuse to play the winner of the other league. The "Fall Classic" would continue uninterrupted until a labor dispute led to its' cancellation in 1994.

The differences between Major League Baseball in 1901 and the brand enjoyed by fans in 2001 didn't happen overnight. Changes occurred slowly, sometimes at a snail's pace, but continued for decades, the cumulative effect resulting in the exciting and fast-paced game witnessed in 2001 (and today). Baseball isn't perfect, and some issues need to be addressed, such as the use of performance-enhancing drugs and eligibility for the Hall-of-Fame, the proliferation of poor umpiring, and escalating ticket prices. But change is a part of life and inevitable. What's happened to America and baseball since the early years of the 20th century testifies to that truth.

Baseball is rich in tradition and history. More-often-than-not, the game has responded well to the challenges it has faced.

Although sometimes resisted at first, intelligent innovation has led to changes that have made the Major League brand of baseball, the fun and interesting past-time it has become.

More changes are on the way.

That's the way of all things in this life.

If history is any indicator, a fascinating future for baseball is *inevitable*.

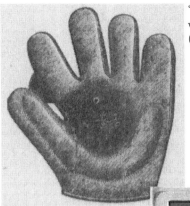

"Pancake" fielding gloves like this were worn in the early days of baseball. (*The Tacoma Times* 1904)

In 1901, Pittsburgh outfielder Ginger Beaumont led his team in home runs with eight. That's right, eight! (US Library of Congress)

BEAUMONT, BOSTON NAT'L

57

Road trips in the early part of the 20th century often included long journeys on trains with no air conditioning and tight compartments. (Flickr)

Major Leaguers in 2001 played in beautiful, well-kept stadiums. Such was not the case in the early days of the 20th century. This helped raise batting averages and home run totals. (Pixabay)

Early 20th century ballparks were smaller with harder and rougher playing surfaces than today. (http://www.ballparks.com/baseball/american/huntin.htm)

Giants manager John McGraw refused to allow his team to play in the 1904 World Series. Back then, participation in the Fall Classic was optional. (US Library of Congress)

—

CHAPTER 7

—

Way Too Soon

War is a wretched fact of life. Armed conflict between nations has occurred frequently throughout history. The United States has been involved in numerous armed engagements, including seven major conflicts since the early years of the 20th century. The number of American military service members who have lost their lives in these major struggles totals just over 400,000 with the potential for more if the U.S goes to war again.

The escapist world of Major League Baseball has not been immune to the reality of modern war. Many players have willingly and effectively served their country in these times of major national and international crises. Sadly, some of these athletes were killed on faraway battlefields, their lives and careers terminated way too soon.

The First World War was fought from 1914 through 1918. The United States entered the conflict in 1917 and, by 1918, had a large expeditionary force fighting on the battlefields of Europe. Approximately 240 active major league baseball players plus numerous ex-big leaguers participated in some way during this bloody conflict. Tragically, two lost their lives in the heat of battle and one from the effects of direct conflict.

The first of these casualties was Eddie Grant, an infielder who played for the Phillies, Reds, and Giants during his ten-year-career. No superstar with a .249 lifetime average, Grant was steady with the glove, finishing in the top four in fielding percentage four times. U.S. Army Captain Grant lost his life on October 5, 1918, during the bloody Meuse-Argonne offensive.

Two days later, another major leaguer was killed in the very same offensive. Robert G. Troy was cut down by German bullets, a sadly ironic end for a man born in Germany in 1888. Nicknamed "Bun," Troy had a brief career as a right-handed pitcher for the Detroit Tigers in 1912. On September 15 of that year, Troy allowed nine hits, and four earned runs over 6.2 innings and was saddled with a loss. It was his only major league appearance, but Bun did enjoy a good five-year minor league career that included two 23-win seasons.

Perhaps the most famous World War I major league combat veteran to lose his life was pitcher Christy Mathewson. The 373 game-winner did not die immediately after being exposed to poison gas in France but for the rest of his life battled serious, chronic respiratory illnesses that culminated in his death from Tuberculosis in 1925. The stylish right-hander was inducted into the Hall-of-Fame in 1936.

Hopes that the "War to End All Wars" would lead to an extended era of global peace were short-lived. By 1939, the world was once again plunged into a multi-continent conflict involving many nations that included major powers such as Germany, Russia, France, Japan, Great Britain, and the United States. Over 500 American major league baseball players served in the armed forces during this deadly conflagration. Stars like Ted Williams,

Joe DiMaggio, Stan Musial, and Bob Feller had their careers interrupted by Uncle Sam's call for men to join America's battle with the Axis nations. Also, many lesser light everyday players, frontline pitchers, and bench warmers saw their baseball careers disrupted by the war. And as in the First World War, numerous other former major leaguers enlisted or were drafted by the U.S. military.

Some baseball people worked as military support personnel and weren't directly involved in combat. Others competed on service baseball teams that traveled to entertain troops. A few engaged in direct warfare with the enemy, on the ground, in the air, or on the sea. Regrettably, two of these combat veteran players lost their lives in battle.

Following the bombing of Pearl Harbor, Elmer Gedeon was drafted by the U.S. Army. A late-season call-up by the Senators in 1939, the 200-pound outfielder hit .200 during a brief five-game career in the majors. In a two-season minor league career, Gedeon batted .265. Possessor of a strong arm, he registered 14 (1939) and 16 (1940) assists as a centerfielder in the minors.

After basic training, Gedeon transferred to the Army Air Force. On March 6, 1945, the Cleveland, Ohio native perished when the B-26B Marauder he was on was shot down on the way to bomb a German target.

Another World War II fatality was Harry O'Neill. His major league was about as brief as one could be. In a single game for the Philadelphia A's in 1939, O'Neill played catcher for one inning in a game against the Tigers. In one at-bat, he failed to get on-base but was errorless behind the plate. While toiling for the then-Pirate minor league affiliate Harrisburg in 1940, the man from Philadelphia batted .238 with one home run in 16 games.

When the United States entered World War II, O'Neill enlisted in the Marines, eventually rising to the rank of First Lieutenant in the Fourth Marine Division. A sniper's bullet cut O'Neill's life short during the bloodstained assault on the island of Iwo Jima in March of 1945.

World War II finally ended in the late summer of 1945. There was peace, but it was tenuous, with tensions running high between one-time allies, the United States and Russia. Communists in China seized control of that country in 1949; America viewed this development as a threat and feared the new anti-Western regime had expansionist aspirations. Led by the United States, a coalition of nations intervened in September 1950 to thwart the invasion of South Korea by the Communist forces of North Korea. In October 1950, Communist Chinese ground forces entered the war in support of their North Korean allies.

By the time the Korean War finally came to an end in the summer of 1953, over 33,000 U.S. service personnel had lost their lives on the Asian peninsula. Of the 366 major league baseball players involved in the conflict, one surrendered his life. Bob Neighbors, who logged seven games with the St. Louis Browns, died at the age of 34 on June 8, 1952. A shortstop, Neighbors batted .182 in eleven plate appearances for the Brownies in September 1939.

Like World War II casualty Elmer Gedeon, Neighbors was killed when the bomber he was a crew member on was shot down. For weeks, the military searched for the three men aboard the aircraft but was unsuccessful in locating any of the bodies.

The United States has fought in four major conflicts since Korea (Vietnam, The Gulf War, Iraq, and Afghanistan). Many have served in these armed struggles, but no major leaguer has died in combat since the early fifties. Bob Neighbors has the distinction of being the last one to sacrifice his life in the heat of battle.

Let's hope he'll be the *final* one.

Boston Red Sox star Ted Williams was one of hundreds of players who joined the armed forces during World War II. (U.S. Marine Corps photo published in 1942)

An exploding shell ended the life of Eddie Grant. He was one of two Major Leaguers who lost their lives during World War I. (The Sporting News)

Grover Cleveland Alexander was plagued with epilepsy after being exposed to a German gas attack during World War I. (U.S. Library of Congress)

Pitcher Bun Troy's time in the majors was brief but he did have a decent career in the minors. (Out of the Park Baseball)

Superstar hitter Stan Musial was one of hundreds of ballplayers who had their careers interrupted by World War II. (Bowman Gum)

Hall-of-Famers Christy Mathewson (left) and Ty Cobb in military uniform. Mathewson suffered from severe respiratory illness for years after being exposed to poison gas in battle. (PD-US/doc)

—

CHAPTER 8

—

Best-Of-The-Worst, 80s Style

The 1980s were a phenomenal decade in the history of Major League Baseball. Fans liked what they saw on the field; overall attendance jumped from about 340 during the 1970s to just under 459 million. After the 1960s, a ten-year-period in which offensive statistics plunged and attendance stagnated, some wondered if Major League baseball had become passé. The exciting 1975 World Series between the Reds and Red Sox helped to partially erase this negative perception, and by the 1980s, the big leagues had regained a respected spot in the consciousness of the sports-following public.

There are several reasons for this resurgence in popularity, but the main cause was a high-caliber on-the-field product. Diverse strategies were on display, and fans appreciated it. People who liked to see the long ball witnessed sluggers like Mike Schmidt and Reggie Jackson slamming home runs regularly. Fans who valued a disciplined and selective approach at the plate had the opportunity to see stars such as George Brett chase the .400-mark one season and four batting titles by Tony Gwynn. Those who appreciated the running game were treated to speedsters like Rickey Henderson and Vince Coleman stealing bunches of bases. Fans love good pitching, and almost every team had at least a guy or two who could "really bring it." *Nine* different pitchers won Cy Young Awards during the decade.

Major League Baseball was fun (again?) for almost everyone associated with the sport in the 1980s.

But not everybody had a jolly good time.

Some teams struggled and were terrible in the 1980s. Fans of these woebegone clubs had little to root for as the losses piled-up, and the playoffs became the impossible dream. However, even during a dreadful season, some players were like genuine diamonds in a sea of zirconium fakes. Rather than allow the pitiful circumstances to blunt their competitive edge, these hardy diamond warriors performed well despite being surrounded by under/or non-productive roster mates. The accomplishments of these players were what lousy team loyalists clung to get them through the summer:

"My team might be in last place, but our clean-up hitter has a good chance to drive-in 100 runs."

"What do you know? Our ace has a chance to win 20 games even though we're 88 games out of first."

"Gee, this young kid just up from the minors has a chance to hit 20 home runs in only half-a-season."

And so on and so forth.

What follows are the recipients of the brand new "I Am Not a Baseball Bozo" (INBB) Awards for the 1980s. These productive guys, who played for the absolute worst teams of the decade, are finally getting a little recognition. The criteria for eligibility are simple:

• The teams these players toiled for must have lost at least 100 games. One-hundred losses are generally considered a benchmark for baseball lousiness.

- Non-pitchers must have appeared in at least 2/3 of the team's 162 games (.67X162 games=108.54games). If a guy hit .300 or something higher but only came to the plate 20 or 30 times, that does not constitute the perseverance needed to garner this prestigious award.
- In the spirit of making things a smidgen more difficult, we are going to round up the 108.54 game number to 109 games as the baseline figure for eligibility.
- To qualify for this prestigious recognition, starting pitchers need to have worked at least 150 innings. Relievers who pitched at least 50 frames for their teams are eligible.
- The player must have performed at a level noticeably higher, statistically, than his teammates during the year considered.
- More than one player from a team and year may win an "INBB" award.

NOTE: The strike season of 1981 was not considered in these evaluations. There were indeed at least two wretched teams that year (Blue Jays, Cubs), but there was always the possibility, however unlikely, that those clubs could have turned things around had the 50-plus games canceled been played. We're sticking with teams that proved their ineptitude over a full schedule and the few players on those teams that persevered.

And now, the Year-By-Year winners of the "INBB" Awards for the 1980s:

1980 *Bruce Bochte (Seattle Mariners 59–103 record).* First baseman Bochte managed to hit .300 with an impressive .381 OBP. He also clubbed 34 doubles and 13 home runs while driving in 78. All this despite playing for a team that finished dead last in batting average, slugging and on-base percentage. Bruce, this "INBB" is for you!

1981 Strike Year-No Award.

1982 *Kent Hrbek (Minnesota Twins 60–102 record)*. Another first baseman. The 22-year-old Hrbek hit 23 home runs, batted .301, and knocked in 92 runs to the delight of the beleaguered Twins' faithful. The 1982 club was young and, within five years, would mature to win the American League pennant and the World Series.

1982 *Tom Brunansky (Minnesota Twins)*. Brunansky (age 21), who gave the Twins and their followers plenty of realistic hope for the future. The outfielder slugged 20 home runs, hit 30 doubles and compiled a lofty .377 OBP. His .848 OPS tied Hrbek for the highest percentage on the team.

1982 *Gary Ward (Minnesota Twins, again)*. Veteran outfielder Gary Ward registered a .289 average to go along with 28 dingers and 91 ribbies (Don't you just love it when we use baseball slang?). 23-year-old Gary Gaetti of the Twins earns an honorable mention with his 25-home run and 84 RBI performance in 1982. A low batting average of .230 kept him from winning an INBB outright.

1982 *Bobby Castillo (Minnesota Twins, by golly!)* Castillo was the only pitcher on the Minnesota staff worth anything in 1982. His line was decent: 13–11, 3.66 ERA, 123 K in 218.2 innings, 1.276 WHIP. The entire staff finished 14th (out of 14 teams) in earned runs, ERA, and walks allowed. They did manage to climb into 13th place in the league in home runs surrendered.

1982 *Dan Driessen (Cincinnati Reds 60–101 record).* Yet another first sacker (This must mean something, but what?) His .269 average was OK, but he did draw 82 walks that contributed to a good .368 on-base percentage. No singles hitter, Driessen ripped 17 home runs and 25 doubles amid the carnage that was a 100-plus loss season for the Red Legs.

1982 *Cesar Cedeno (Cincinnati Reds).* Fine .289 average and 57 RBIs on a team that didn't put a whole lot of runners on base ahead of him. His on-base percentage was a respectable .346. A top-notch defensive outfielder, Cedeno committed only three errors in 132 games.

1982 *Dave Concepcion (Cincinnati Reds).* One of the last vestiges of Cincy's "Big Red Machine" of the 1970s, the 34-year-old infielder produced the second highest batting average for a regular on the team (.287) and continued to make all the plays, finishing third in the league in overall fielding percentage (.977).

1982 *Mario Soto (Cincinnati Reds).* His so-so 14–13 record was due mainly to lack of support from teammates and not his pitching. No siree. In 257 innings, Soto fanned 274 and allowed only 202 hits. His excellent ERA and WHIP numbers (2.79 and 1.060) helped place Mario among baseball's elite hurlers in 1982. Reds fans must have been grateful for Mr. Soto's performance. The rest of Cincy's rotation went a combined 22–44 as the team claimed their spot in the NL Western Division cellar.

1983 *Steve Henderson (Seattle Mariners, 60–102).* Can't blame that record on the man from Houston, TX. Henderson delivered a .294 AVG and .356 OBP for a woeful Mariners club. The outfielder slashed 32 doubles and plated 55 teammates. His performance really shines because Seattle finished last that season in runs, hits, average, on-base percentage, slugging, and total bases. Also, in 1983, Matt Young (Seattle Mariners). The ace of a mediocre pitching staff, Young was one of the league's better pitchers in 1983. His 11–15 record belied a total stat package that included a 3.27 era, just 178 hits in 203 innings pitched, 130 K, and a 1.262 WHIP. An honorable mention goes to infielder Pat Putnam of the Mariners who drilled 19 home runs and knocked in 67 runs in 1983.

1984 No 100-loss teams.

1985 *Joe Orsulak (Pittsburgh Pirates 57–104).* Over 121 games played, the singles-hitting outfielder logged a .300 AVG, .342 OBP, and stole 24 bases. Not bad stats on a team that collectively hit .255.

1985 *Johnny Ray (Pittsburgh Pirates).* Veteran second baseman pleased Pirate faithful by knocking in 70 runs. Ray drilled 33 doubles and struck out only 24 times in 652 plate appearances.

1985 *Rick Reuschel (Pittsburgh Pirates).* While just about everything in the Steel City was crashing in around him, the chubby one put in an excellent season. His record was 14–8 with a fine 2.27 ERA and a tiny 1.057 WHIP. In 194 innings, he surrendered just 153 hits and struck out 130.

1985 *Cecilio Guante (Pittsburgh Pirates).* A richly deserved INBB Award for this fellow. In 1985, Guante posted a 2.72 ERA, allowed just 84 hits in 109 innings, fanned 92, and finished with a 1.138 WHIP. As a staff, the Pirates finished at or near the bottom in almost every category.

1985 *Tony Bernazard (Cleveland Indians 60–102).* The Tribe second baseman earns an INBB based on his .274 AVG, .361 OBP, 59 RBI, and 17 steals. His 11 home runs were quite noticeable on a club that didn't hit many long balls; Cleveland finished 13th out of 14 teams in home runs (116).

1985 *Julio Franco (Cleveland Indians).* This guy persevered through his club's mounting losses by hitting .288 and driving in 99 runs. Despite the lack of home run power, the Indians' problem in 1985 wasn't really their offense; they finished fourth in the league in hitting (.265) and third in stolen bases (132).

1985 *Brett Butler (Cleveland Indians).* A genuinely outstanding player who was highly productive during a 17-year-career in the big leagues. The 665,181 long-suffering fans that went through the turnstiles at Municipal Stadium in 1985 had the privilege of watching one of the game's best. Throughout that disastrous campaign, the swift Butler hit .311, swatted 14 triples, and stole 44 bases. His .377 OBP was impressive, and 50 RBIs were outstanding for a lead-off hitter. If anyone deserves an INBB Award for the 1980s, it was Brett Butler in 1985.

1985 *Bert Blyleven (Cleveland Indians).* Over 179 innings of work, Blyleven fanned 129 batters, not a bad total for a staff that finished last overall in strikeouts. His record was only 9–11, but that sort of thing often happens to good pitchers who toil for poor teams. With a 3.26 ERA and 15 complete games, he deserved better but sometimes reality *bites*. Nobody else on the team had an ERA below 3.92, and his fellow starting pitchers sported earned run averages of 4.90, 5.34, 6.01, and 6.68.

1985 *Chris Brown (San Francisco Giants 62–100).* With a not-so-bad .271 batting average, an equally not-so-bad .345 OBP, almost-impressive 16 home runs, and kind of-decent 61 RBIs, the Giants third baseman earns an INBB. But just *barely.*

1985 *Chili Davis (San Francisco Giants).* His line: .270 AVG, .349 OBP, 13 HRs, and 56 RBIs. Just like teammate Brown, his sort-of-OK stats lifted him just above mediocrity and earn him this coveted award.

1985 *Mike Krukow (San Francisco Giants).* Never mind the 8–11 record (see the Bert Blyleven comments), check out the 150 Ks in 194 innings pitched, 1.156 WHIP and decent 3.38 ERA. Another solid pitcher stuck on a crappy team.

1985 *Scott Garrelts (San Francisco Giants).* One of baseball's best relievers in 1985, Garrelts allowed just 76 hits in 105 innings pitched and surrendered just two home runs. His save total of 13 would have almost assuredly been higher had he pitched for a better team. Mark Davis of the 1985 Giants deserves an honorable mention despite a 5–12 record. In 114 innings, Davis struck out 113 and allowed only 89 hits. Another honorable mention goes to Giants outfielder Jeff Leonard who cracked 17 home runs, drove in 62, and swiped 11 bases in 1985. A middling .241 batting average keeps him from winning an INBB Award outright.

1986 No 100-loss turkeys, so no INBB awarded.

1987 *Julio Franco (Cleveland Indians 61–101).* Back in the 1980s, Cleveland was one of the sorriest franchises in baseball. Since we just finished a rundown on another inept Indians team (1985), we're going to keep this one short. Notwithstanding their 101 losses, the Tribe did have a few guys deserving of an INBB. With a .319 AVG, .389 OBP, and 33 steals, Franco was one of our "chosen" few. There were other Indian "honorees" in 1987:

- Joe Carter, who hit 32 home runs, knocked-in 106 and stole 31 bases.
- Brook Jacoby also homered 32 times to go along with a .300 AVG and .387 OBP.
- Cory Snyder beat Carter and Jacoby in the HR department with his 33 round-trippers. The Indians' right fielder also compiled 82 RBIs.
- Designated Hitter Pat Tabler plated 86 teammates on his way to a final .307 AVG.
- Lead-off man Brett Butler had another outstanding season in 1987 (.295 AVG, .399 OBP, 33 steals) to cop his second INBB Award.

Once again, as in 1985, the Tribe's problem in 1987 was not their offense. Their pitching staff stunk with their "ace" Tom Candiotti going 7–18 and registering a whopping 4.78 ERA. The only bright spot was reliever Doug Jones who went 6–5 with a good 3.15 ERA. The rest of the guys in the bullpen had ERA figures ranging from 4.65 to 5.67. Doug Jones earns an INBB Award for his efforts.

1988 *Eddie Murray (Baltimore Orioles 54–107).* You can't blame the once-proud O's collapse in 1988 on Murray. Steady Eddie blasted 28 home runs to go along with a .284 average and .361 OBP.

Also, in 1988, Cal Ripken, Jr. (Baltimore Orioles). It wasn't Junior's fault, either. His line: .264 AVG, .372 OBP, 23 HRs, 81 RBIs. It was typical Ripken-at-his-peak production during a very un-Oriole like season. And let's not forget Joe Orsulak of the Orioles. Outfielder Joe earns his second INBB with a good

.288 average and respectable .331 OBP in 1988. Not bad figures on a club with an overall average of .238 and OBP of .305, both of which ranked last in the American League. Baltimore also finished 14th out of 14 teams in hits, runs, and slugging.

1988 *Gerald Perry (Atlanta Braves 54–106).* Perry's efforts in Atlanta's ill-fated 1988 season earned him his one and only berth on the NL All-Star team. The left-handed swinging Perry batted .300, drove in 74 runs, and stole 29 bases. He is also the only Brave to cop an INBB Award for his team's disastrous campaign. However, two of his teammates deserve honorable mention:

• Second baseman Ron Gant (24 HRs, 8 triples, 60 RBIs in 1988). A poor .317 OBP and 118 K were deciding factors in denying Mr. Gant the award. He was also brutal in the field, leading the league in errors at second. A rookie in 1988, Gant would eventually be moved to the outfield where he would thrive and become a top-notch player.

• Dale Murphy was on the backside of his productive career in 1988 and only hit .226 and fanned 125 times. But he did crash 24 home runs, 35 doubles, and knocked-in 77 Braves. Had that average and OBP (.313) been a lot higher, the former first-round pick would have snared an INBB outright instead of an honorable mention.

Two hurlers on the 1988 team did give the fans occasional glimpses of what good major league pitching actually-looks-like. For their efforts on the mound, these two Braves have earned an INBB Award:

• Jose Alvarez (2.99 ERA, 88 hits allowed and 81 K in 102 innings)

• Paul Assenmacher (3.06 ERA, 72 hits allowed and 71 K in 79 innings)

1989 *Lou Whitaker (Detroit Tigers, 59–103).* A holdover from the 1984 Detroit juggernaut that captured the AL pennant and World Championship, Whitaker kept on producing despite the 1988 club's profound lack-of-success. The seasoned second sacker's batting average (.251) was unremarkable, but among his 128 hits were 28 home runs and 21 doubles. His OBP was very good at .361, and he drove in 85 runs. Give that dude one of them there INBB awards!

1989 *Gary Pettis (Detroit Tigers).* Speedster Pettis walked 84 times, a figure which contributed heavily to an excellent .375 OBP. Any time the man got on base, he was a threat to go and swiped 43 bases (fourth-best in the league). A nothing-special .257 batting average is countered with a fourth Gold Glove Award for his work in the outfielder.

1989 *Mike Henneman (Detroit Tigers).* The tall right-handed reliever was the *only* pitcher on the 1989 Tiger staff with a winning record (11–4). He allowed only 4 home runs over his 60 appearances while compiling an OK 3.70 ERA. There was also a Detroit player who should be recognized with an honorable mention: Staff ace Frank Tanana went 10–14 with a 3.58 ERA. He struck out 147 in 223 innings pitched, hurled 6 complete games, and finished the season with an adequate 1.346 WHIP. Granted, it's not an impressive line for the then-35-year-old hurler but much better than the rest of Detroit rotation that went a combined 20–43. The starter with the next lowest ERA was Kevin Ritz, with a bloated 4.38.

That's it. The selections for the decade of the 1980s are complete. You may disagree with some of these choices and perhaps can think of other players that you believe should have had an INBB Award or honorable mention bestowed upon them. The purpose of this exercise was to recognize guys who could have tanked it and gone-through-the motions while playing on a bad club destined to lose 100 games or more. If you think players on poor teams would never give less-than-100 percent, keep in mind that pitcher Jim Bouton once said that the Yankees did that exact thing in 1965. As the team struggled and fell farther behind first place in the standings, Bouton believed that most of his teammates basically threw-in-the-towel mentally, resulting in a second division finish for New York.

Human nature being what it is, it could happen. And although few would admit it, there's a good chance it happens more often than baseball idealists would care to imagine.

So, even the faithful followers of Major League Baseball's "never-rans" had a few things to cheer about in the 1980s. Apparently, none of the players honored with an INBB Award or an honorable mention "threw-in-the-towel" mentally while their club swirled down the baseball hopper.

Congratulations go out to all the players in the 1980s who didn't allow dire circumstances to adversely affect their performance.

Thanks go out to all of you.

Your professionalism has not been forgotten!

First Baseman Eddie Murray hit 28 home runs during Baltimore's nightmare 1988 season. (Baseball card from 1977 via tradingcarddb.com)

Slick-fielding shortstop Dave Concepcion hit .287 in 1982 to garner a INBB. (Hostess via tradingcarddb.com)

Hurler Rick Reuschel captured a highly coveted INBB award for his efforts in 1985. (Jewel Foods via tradingcarddb.com)

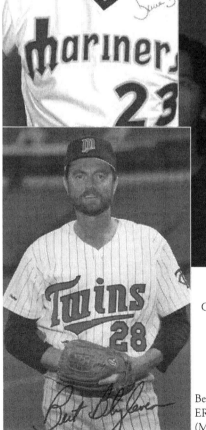

Bruce Bochte's .300 average and .381 OBP in 1980 earned him an INBB. (Fred Meyer via tradingcarddb.com)

Versatile outfielder Brett Butler earned two INBB awards in the 1980s. (Gabriel Cervantes/Creative Commons Attribution-Share Alike 3.0 Unported)

Bert Blyleven won an INBB with a 3.26 ERA and 15 complete games in 1985. (Minnesota Twins via tradingcarddb.com)

Second baseman Lou Whitaker's performance was one of the few bright spots in a dismal 1989 Tiger season. ((77) Tiger Stadium (Lou Whitaker) 8.81/ Creative Commons)

Tanana pitched well-enough in 1989 to snag an INBB Honorable Mention. (https://www.flickr.com/photos/piedmont_fossil/4037029183/ Creative Commons Attribution 2.0 Generic)

CHAPTER 9

The Bill Bergen Line?

One of the most famous phrases in baseball is "The Mendoza Line." Named after Mario Mendoza, who played in the majors in the 1970s and early 1980s, it's the mythical line used to describe batting averages that are at the microscopic .200 level and below. Now part of popular culture, the saying is sometimes used to describe mediocrity in politics, finance, and entertainment.

Who was Mario Mendoza?

Was he *that* bad?

Signed by the Pirates as an amateur free agent in 1970, Mendoza made his major league debut in April 1974. As a back-up shortstop, Mendoza hit .221 in 91 games that year, a figure well above the "line" later named after him. Also, he drove in 15 runs in 163 at-bats, not a bad figure for a guy who was supposed to be an automatic out.

Mendoza's batting stats over the next four years probably did more to earn him infamy than anything else. In limited playing time, the slick-fielding Mexican hit .180, .185, .198, and .218. The most at-bats he compiled in a season during this time was 92 in 1976, but he also drove-in 12 that year. Projected out over 500 at-bats, that's the equivalent of a respectable 55 runs-batted-in, so Mendoza could hurt a pitcher if he didn't bear down.

Pittsburgh traded Mario to the Mariners after the 1978 season. Given a chance to play 148 games in 1979, Mendoza hit under "his" line (.198), but among his safeties were 10 doubles and three triples. He also was eighth in the American League in sacrifice hits with 14.

None of these numbers would make one push for Mendoza's inclusion into the Hall-of-Fame, but they show that, even at his "worst," he wasn't the offensive zero he's sometimes made out to be.

Mendoza's best year at the plate was 1980. In 277 at-bats, he hit .245 (!), including three triples and two (!) home runs. His slugging average of .310 in 1980 was the highest of his career.

Proving 1980 was no fluke, the shortstop hit .231 in 1981 for the Mariners. Over 229 at-bats, Mendoza knocked-in 22 runs, not exactly Babe Ruth numbers but OK for a back-up infielder.

Traded to the Rangers after the 1981 campaign, Mendoza saw limited action early in the 1982 season (12 games) and was released in June. Rather than seek employment with another major league team, Mario went home to play in the Mexican League for eight-of-the-next nine years (he spent the 1983 season with the Pirates AAA team).

Mendoza was inducted into the Mexican Baseball Hall-of-Fame in 2000.

The whole "Mendoza Line" thing seems even more unjust when you consider the fact that there have been players with *actual* sub-.200 career batting averages. Let's compare Mendoza's career stats with three examples relevant to this discussion:

- Mendoza (1974 to 1982 Pirates, Mariners, Rangers)
  686 games, .215 AVG, .245 OBP
- Bill Bergen (1901 to 1911 Dodger, Reds)
  947 games, .170 AVG, .194 OBP
- Ray Oyler (1965 to 1970 Tigers, Pilots, Angels)
  542 games, .175 AVG, .258 OBP
- Mike Ryan (1964 to 1974 Red Sox, Phillies, Pirates)
  636 games, .193 AVG, .252 OBP

As you can see, there have been three guys who "out-Mendoza'd" Mendoza when it comes to fecklessness at the plate. Why did fate choose the slick-fielding Mexican for baseball infamy? It wasn't fair or completely accurate back then, and it still isn't today. The phrase "The Mendoza Line" should be deep-sixed, perhaps replaced by "The Bergen Line." Bill Bergen may have been the all-time worst hitter in major league baseball history with that .170 average over an eleven-year career. The reason why he hung around so long was the fact that he was an excellent fielding catcher with a .972 percentage and an average of 47% base stealing kills over 162 games. The kills are particularly impressive considering he played during the Dead Ball Era when teams attempted to steal a lot more frequently than they do in the 21st century.

The other two, Ryan and Oyler, were also very good fielders and helped save runs with their gloves. They certainly didn't hang around for several seasons because of their batting prowess.

Based on Mario Mendoza's career stats, the phrase "The Mendoza Line" is a bum rap. Given the opportunity to play more-than-a-handful of games in three seasons (1979 through 1981), Mendoza responded with two years of averages well-over the "line." Even when he hit .198 in 1979, he drove-in a few runs and ripped a fair amount of extra-base hits. And through-it-all, his fielding was never in question.

STEALING FIRST AND OTHER OLD-TIME BASEBALL STORIES

If Mario Mendoza had been a total stiff, he would have never lasted nine-years in the major leagues. The Pirates had good teams in the 1970s and were in the playoff hunt every year Mendoza was on the club. They couldn't afford to carry any player who couldn't help them.

They kept Mendoza for five seasons despite low averages.

Since Mendoza had a lifetime major-league batting average of .215 (not sub .200) and others managed to hit .200 or below, the phrase "The Mendoza Line" is inaccurate and unfair.

Mario Mendoza was not a great player, but he wasn't a joke, either.

He was a light-hitting gloveman, and there have been plenty of them in baseball history.

With a .170 lifetime average, Bill Bergen is probably the worst hitter of all-time. (U.S. Library of Congress)

Infielder Ray Oyler had a lifetime batting average 40 points lower than Mario Mendoza. (Seattle Pilots via tradingcarddb.com)

Mike Ryan had a lifetime batting average of .193. It was his outstanding defensive skills that kept him the majors for 11 years. (Boston Red Sox via tradingcarddb.com)

A young and slim Babe Ruth. Mendoza was no Bambino but he wasn't the worst hitter of all-time either. (Mears Auctions)

—

CHAPTER 10

—

Walk This Way

Is the number of walks drawn by a team or player a reliable barometer of success or lack thereof? Some argue that making contact and putting the ball in play is more beneficial to a team than waiting out a free pass. Personally, I've had a bias towards the value of the walk, assuming-that-the-best clubs and players racked-up more free passes than the bottom-dwellers in both categories. I've decided to conduct a mini-challenge of my bias. So that this article doesn't become cumbersome and treacly, I will limit its' scope by looking at a few league champions to see if they drew more walks than clubs with the worst records. Also, I'll compare some batting champs with guys who had extreme difficulty getting base hits to see if there were any significant differences between the two groups.

What follows is not an exhaustive treatise on the value of the free pass. I'm looking for a general trend or trends here and won't pretend that my findings are conclusive.

The following chart contains the walk totals for every pennant winner for the ten years 2007 through 2016, including season records and where the teams ranked in their league for the number of bases-on-balls:

2007 Red Sox 96–66 689 walks (1st)
2007 Rockies 90–73 622 walks (2nd)
2008 Rays 97–65 626 walks (2nd)
2008 Phillies 92–70 586 walks (5th)
2009 Yankees 103–59 663 walks (1st)
2009 Phillies 93–69 589 walks (7th)
2010 Rangers 90–72 511 walks (8th)
2010 Giants 92–70 487 walks (13th)
2011 Rangers 96–66 475 walks (8th)
2011 Cardinals 90–72 542 walks (3rd)
2012 Tigers 88–74 511 walks (5th)
2012 Giants 94–68 483 walks (7th)
2013 Red Sox 97–65 581 walks (2nd)
2013 Cardinals 97–65 481 walks (5th)
2014 Royals 89–73 380 walks (15th)
2014 Giants 88–74 427 walks (11th)
2015 Royals 95–67 383 walks (15th)
2015 Mets 90–72 488 walks (7th)
2016 Indians 94–67 531 walks (4th)
2016 Cubs 103–58 656 walks (1st)

These twenty pennant winners amassed 10,711 walks over the ten years being considered. The average walk totals per team per season was 535.55 (10,711 walks divided by 20 teams=535.55). When it comes to overall seasonal league walk placement, the median figure is 6.1, meaning these successful clubs ranked slightly higher than sixth in bases-on-balls (122 places divided by 20 teams=6.1).

STEALING FIRST AND OTHER OLD-TIME BASEBALL STORIES

To be honest, I thought the overall and seasonal walk totals would be higher and the average placement to be closer to the top (for the greatest number of walks). The pennant winners did draw a lot of free passes but not as many as I expected.

Next, I'd like to examine totals for the two worst teams, record-wise each year, for the period 2007 to 2016:

2007 Rays 66–96 545 walks (5th)
2007 Pirates 68–94 463 walks (16th)
2008 Mariners 61–101 417 walks (13th)
2008 Nationals 59–102 534 walks (12th)
2009 Orioles 64–98 517 walks (11th)
2009 Nationals 59–103 617 walks (2nd)
2010 Mariners 61–101 459 walks (13th)
2010 Pirates 57–105 463 walks (15th)
2011 Twins 63–99 440 walks (13th)
2011 Astros 56–106 401 walks (16th)
2012 Twins 66–96 505 walks (6th)
2012 Astros 55–107 463 walks (12th)
2013 Astros 51–111 426 walks (12th)
2013 Marlins 62–100 432 walks (12th)
2014 Rangers 67–95 417 walks (11th)
2014 Diamondbacks 64–98 398 walks (14th)
2015 Athletics 68–94 475 walks (8th)
2015 Phillies 63–99 387 walks (14th)
2016 Twins 59–103 513 walks (5th)
2016 Padres 68–94 449 walks (13th)

The twenty last-place finishers from 2007 through 2016 compiled a total of 9,321 bases-on-balls, with a seasonal average of 466.05 walks per team (9,321 walks divided by 20 teams=466.05). Cellar dwellers ranked an average of 11.15 in their leagues for total walks (222 total places divided by 20=11.15). Once again, I was a bit surprised by the numbers. I strongly suspected that poor clubs drew fewer walks than good ones, but I thought the doormats would have an even fewer number of bases on balls than they did.

Next, let's look at individual performances. Good hitters frequently are patient at the plate, i.e., they don't swing at a lot of pitches out of the strike zone. Some of the finest hitters of all-time have had elevated lifetime on-base percentages, thanks in part to walk totals significantly higher than those less successful. Guys like Ted Williams (.344 AVG, 144 walks, .482 OBP), Babe Ruth (.342 AVG, 133 walks, .474 OBP), and Mickey Mantle (.298 AVG, 117 walks, .421 OBP) racked-up a high number of bases-on-balls. More recent stars such as Frank Thomas (.301 AVG, 116 walks, .419 OBP), Chipper Jones (.303 AVG, 98 walks, .401 OBP), and Todd Helton (.316 AVG, 96 walks, .414 OBP) also seemed to have that "camera eye" during their time in the batter's box. And although their walk counts weren't quite as impressive, the 2016 batting champions, Jose Altuve (.338 AVG, 60 walks, .396 OBP) and DJ LeMahieu (.348AVG, 66 walks, .416 OBP) registered good totals for the season.

What about the fellows who weren't nearly as successful with the bat during their major league careers? The infamous Mario Mendoza (.215 AVG, 12 walks, .245 OBP) immediately comes to mind and has close competition for hitting ineptness from Johnny LeMaster (.222 AVG, .38 walks, .277 OBP), J.P. Arencibia (.212 AVG, 29 walks, .258 OBP), and Manny Alexander (.231 AVG, 23 walks, .282 OBP). Each of these gentlemen spent several years in the majors and couldn't have been total zeros; otherwise, they would have been banished from big-league rosters quickly. But they weren't good hitters, and the stats seem to indicate that they weren't particularly adept at laying-off bad pitches or couldn't handle a ball in the strike zone. It's also likely that these four, along with countless others who have posted similar averages and walk totals, weren't quite as talented/or intelligent than the guys who compiled gaudy numbers.

A comparison of the four players with the highest averages with the four lowest in 2015 and 2016 is interesting. Batting champions Jose Altuve, DJ LeMahieu, Miguel Cabrera, and Dee Gordon drew a total of 228 walks between them over the two seasons for an average of 57 walks (228 divided by 4=57). The four lowest (Danny Espinosa, Alex Gordon, Jimmy Rollins, and Logan Morrison) walked a total of 203 times for an average of 50.75 walks (203 divided by 4=50.75). The Champs walked more but not so much more as to cause one to say, "Wow! What a difference!" After seeing this, I wondered if walks aren't quite as important to success as I had previously believed

I decided to look at a slightly larger sample from the years 1910 to 2010). I selected batting champions from random years during that period with their walk totals:

2004   Ichiro Suzuki .372 AVG, 49 walks

1994   Tony Gwynn .394 AVG. 48 walks

1980   George Brett .380 AVG, 58 walks

1970   Rico Carty .366 AVG, 77 walks

1961   Norm Cash .361 AVG, 124 walks

1957   Ted Williams .388 AVG, 119 walks

1941   Ted Williams .406 AVG, 147 walks

1930   Bill Terry .401 AVG, 47 walks

1924   Rogers Hornsby .424 AVG, 89 walks

1911   Ty Cobb .420 AVG, 44 walks

Next, I took a sample of guys over the same period that had low batting averages. Each of them was a) regulars or b) semi-regulars or c) bench players who made at least 350 plate appearances. Here are those figures:

2000 Kevin Jordan .220 AVG, 17 walks
1994 Matt Walbeck .204 AVG, 17 walks
1986 Rafael Santana .218 AVG, 36 walks
1978 Luis Gonzalez .223 AVG, 34 walks
1963 Bobby Wine .214 AVG, 14 walks
1956 Ted Kazanski .211 AVG, 20 walks
1947 Howie Shultz .223 AVG, 21 walks
1936 Skeeter Newsome .225 AVG, 25 walks
1920 Ray Powell .225 AVG, 44 walks
1909 Bill Bergen .163 AVG, 10 walks

No need to crunch the numbers when comparing these two groups. Even a cursory look tells us that the batting champions had higher walk totals than the players who struggled at the plate.

Overall, the batting champions did draw noticeably higher base-on-ball totals than their less-successful brethren. In recent years the gap between the best and worst teams doesn't seem to be as wide as it was in past decades. For the most part, the results were close to what I suspected when I started, but I didn't want to assume anything. For me, part of the fun of being a stats wonk is being open to changing my mind when presented with a logical, numbers-based opposing argument.

This time, my mind wasn't changed.

Next time I examine an issue, it just might.

Hall-of-Famer Ted Williams averaged an incredible 143 walks-per-season over a 19-year career. (*Baseball Digest* 1949)

Tigers star Norm Cash drew 124 walks while winning the 1961 American League batting title. (Detroit Tigers via tradingcarddb.com)

When Rogers Hornsby hit a lofty .424 in 1924, he also drew 89 walks. Some guys don't even get 89 *hits* in a season... (*TIME* Magazine cover, 9 July 1928)

CHAPTER 11

The Cinderella Team That Almost Was (Just use your imagination . . .)

The 1973 Philadelphia Phillies finished last in the National League Eastern Division with a 71–91 record. In most seasons, that kind of performance would have buried them deep in the standings, but the Phils finished a not-so-horrific 11½ games out of first. The 2016 edition of the Phillies compiled an identical record and trailed division-leading Washington by 24 games at the season's end. The Nationals won going away in 2016, finishing eight games ahead of the second-place Mets.

Such was not the case in 1973. All the teams in the Eastern Division struggled that year, and throughout September, it was a legitimate five-team race with only the Phillies fading down over the last four weeks. The Mets, who on August 15th were in last place and 1½ games behind Philadelphia, got red-hot down the stretch and won the division.

Only 5½ games out on August 20th and 6 after play on the 31st, Philly was in the hunt for a while. Despite having several good-to-decent players, their obvious weaknesses doomed them once September rolled around. But as ridiculous as it might sound, the Phillies might have been a shocking "Cinderella" club had one thing been different.

That one difference centered around pitcher Steve Carlton.

In 1972, Carlton was the best pitcher in the Major Leagues. While toiling for one of the worst teams in baseball, he went 27–10 with a 1.96 ERA. Over 346 innings, he fanned 310 and completed 30 games. For his herculean efforts, "Lefty" captured the first of four Cy Young awards he would garner in his career. With a nasty slider and overpowering fastball, he was nearly unhittable. It's scary to think what his record might have been had he not pitched for a Phillies club that finished with a woeful record of 59–97.

An injury hampered Carlton in 1973, and his record slumped to 13–20, and his ERA ballooned to 3.90. His control suffered with his walk total jumping from 87 in 1972 to 113 in 1973. Number 32 also served-up 12 more home runs than the previous season (29–17). It was one of the worst seasons in the Hall-of-Fame pitcher's career.

Although the 1973 Phillies weren't great, they were improved over 1972. The Phillies clubbed 134 home runs as compared to 98 in 1972. The team batting average rose 13 points, slugging jumped 27 points, and OBP was higher by eight points.

Overall, the 1972 and 1973 starting rotations were roughly equivalent in performance. However, the 1972 stats are somewhat skewered by Carlton's phenomenal season. After Carlton's 1.97 ERA, the two lowest numbers in the starting rotation were 4.26

and 4.36. Carlton fanned over 300 batters in 1972, no one else on the staff reached the 100 K mark. No Philly starter approached Lefty's .993 WHIP with the closest figure being Ken Reynolds's 1.354. And reliever Darrell Brandon's seven wins was second on the team to Carlton's 27.

Take Steve Carlton of 1972 out of the equation, and you see that 1973's starters were better. Hard-throwing Wayne Twitchell logged a 13–9 record, 2.50 ERA and 169 K in 223 innings. Left-hander Ken Brett also went 13–9 with a decent 3.44 ERA and 111 K in just over 211 innings of work. Despite a high 4.88 ERA, Jim Lonborg battled his way to 13 wins with 106 K in 199 innings. Rookie Dick Ruthven was still learning the hitters (6–9, 4.21 ERA) but was an upgrade over 1972's fifth starter Billy Champion (4–14, 5.09 ERA).

Offensively, second-year man Greg Luzinski helped fuel Philly's attack with 29 home runs and 97 RBIs. Veteran Bill Robinson smacked 25 dingers, Del Unser hit .289 and played an excellent center field. Rookie Mike Schmidt struggled at times at the plate (.196 AVG) but managed to crash 18 home runs. Philadelphia had some potent weapons, so Carlton's drastic one-year decline can be squarely blamed on physical problems and not pitching for a hopeless bunch of losers.

Had the big guy been healthy in 1973, it would not have been unreasonable to expect him to win at least twenty games, perhaps more. Including his incredible performance in 1972, Carlton logged 20-win seasons five times:

1971 20–9
1972 27–10
1976 23–10
1980 24–9
1982 23–11

What might have happened had Carlton compiled stats like 1972 for the Phillies in 1973? A case can be made that Philly just might have snuck off with the Eastern Division title. At the very least, they would have been right there, in the thick of things, at the end.

Before you laugh and write this essay off as the rantings of a crazy person, consider the following:

- All the teams in the Eastern Division struggled to play winning baseball that season. The New York Mets captured the crown with just an 82–79 record. The only other club to play at least .500 baseball was the second place St. Louis Cardinals, who finished 81–81.

- In 37 decisions during the 1972 campaign, Steve Carlton's winning percentage was .730. Had he repeated that winning percentage over his 33 decisions in 1973, he would have won 24 games (.730 X 33=24.09). Subtract that 24 from the number of decisions (33), and you get 9, which would be the number of losses suffered.

- If the man from Miami, Florida had gone 24–9 in 1973, here's what the top two teams in the division would have been at the close of play on the last day of the season:
  New York Mets 82–79____
  Philadelphia Phillies 82–80 0.5 GB
  (NOTE: In this fantasy scenario, we only imagine the Mets finishing with the same "real" 1973 record. Had Carlton delivered 24 wins that season, the won-lost records of the other four teams in the division probably would have been slightly different unless all of Carlton's extra 11 victories were racked-up against Western Division clubs. That would have been unlikely.)

- The "real" Phillies went 71–91 in 1973. Subtract Carlton's actual 13–20 record from the totals, and you get 58 wins

STEALING FIRST AND OTHER OLD-TIME BASEBALL STORIES

and 71 losses. Now add an imagined Carlton record of 24–9, and the result is an 82–80 record for the Phillies (58+24=82, 71+9=80). The Mets, who had played 161 games to that point, would have been forced to make-up an earlier cancellation. Had they lost that contest, in this fictional scenario, Tug McGraw and company would have finished in a flat-footed tie with Philadelphia. A one-game playoff for the division title between the Phillies and the Mets would have followed, and in a single game, anything can happen.

- Even if Carlton had "only" won 20 games, that still would have put the Phillies right in the middle of things during a hectic last week-and-a-half that saw five teams with a legitimate shot at finishing in first. Twenty wins for the Hall-of-Fame lefty would have resulted in a 78–82 record for the Phillies, 4.5 games behind the Mets,

- The Mets had a much-better pitching staff in 1973 than the 71–91 Phillies. Led by Tom Seaver (19–10, 2.08 ERA), Jerry Koosman (14–15, 2.84 ERA) and Jon Matlack (3.20 ERA), the New Yorkers caught fire In September and leap-frogged over the rest of the division to finish in first place.

- But the "real" Phillies were a better club offensively than the 1973 Mets. They had a higher team batting average (.249 to .246), better slugging average (.371 to .338), compiled more doubles (218 to198), triples (29 to 24) and clubbed more home runs (134 to 85). Philly stole 51 bases to 27 for New York.

- Both teams did a decent job of making the plays in the field. The Mets finished fourth in the league in fielding percentage (.980) while the Phillies ranked fifth (.973).

The point of the preceding comparisons is to point out that the division-winning Mets were not vastly superior statistically to the Phils. Yogi Berra did have a top-quality pitching staff at his disposal, much better than Danny Ozark's. But considering the pedestrian performance of the teams in the division in 1973, is it all that strange to wonder how the last-place Phillies might have fared had their ace, Steve Carlton, been at the top of his game?

Of course, it didn't happen. The Mets were smoking-hot at the end of the season and went on to beat the Reds in the playoffs before taking the eventual 1973 World Champion A's to seven games in the World Series.

Over the next three seasons, the Phillies steadily improved and would capture their first NL East title in 1976.

It's a tribute to Carlton's grittiness and mental toughness that he was able to work through the pain and win 13 games in 1973. Had he been healthy, that first Divisional title might have arrived a little sooner for Philadelphia.

Ace Steve Carlton's off year in 1973 may have cost the Phillies a shot at the playoffs. (Hostess via tradingcarddb.com)

Hall-of-Fame catcher Yogi Berra. He managed a 1973 Mets team that was buried in last place in August to the National League pennant. (1953 Bowman Gum)

Rookie Mike Schmidt powered 18 homeruns while holding down third base for the 1973 Phils. (KG Graphics via tradingcarddb.com)

Jim Lonborg. After being acquired in a trade, the former Cy Young Award winner won 13 games for the Phillies in 1973. (Boston Red Sox via tradingcarddb.com)

Tom "Terrific" Seaver won 19 games for the 1973 National League Champs. (Hostess via tradingcarddb.com)

—

—

CHAPTER 12

How Do You Win 111 Games and Then Get Swept in the World Series?

It's always puzzled me how the Cleveland Indians were dispatched so quickly in the 1954 World Series. Their opponent, the New York Giants, was very good and had the tools to win the seven-game match-up. But a four-game sweep? Based on the Indians' regular-season performance, it's hard to believe they didn't win at least a game or two.

Cleveland thundered through their schedule with a phenomenal 111–43 record, besting the second-place Yankees by eight games. The Bronx Bombers finished with a better record in 1954 than they had in the previous five seasons, all pennant-winning campaigns. The Tribe's 111 wins were the American League record until the Yankees won 114 in 1998. The Mariners topped that three years later with 116 wins.

To finish ahead of an outstanding Yankee team, the Indians needed plenty of excellent performances, and they got them. At the plate, third baseman Al Rosen (.300 AVG, .404 OBP, 24 HRs, 102 RBIs). Centerfielder Larry Doby (.272 AVG, .364 OBP, 32 HRs, 126 RBIs) and second baseman Bobby Avila (.341 AVG, .402 OBP, 15 HRs, 67 RBIs) were the hub of a strong attack that led the league in runs scored. Mid-season acquisition Vic Wertz added 15 fence-clearing blasts and 48 runs-batted-in over 337 plate appearances.

The 1954 Indians not only could hit well but could also pitch with the best-of-them. As-a-matter of fact, they had one of the finest single-season starting rotations of all time. Check these impressive stats:

Early Wynn 23–11, 2.73 ERA, 1.138 WHIP
Bob Lemon 23–7, 2.72 ERA, 1.239 WHIP
Mike Garcia 19–8, 2.64 ERA, 1.125 WHIP
Bob Feller 13–3, 3.09 ERA, 1.186 WHIP
Art Houtteman 13–3, 3.35 ERA, 1.367 WHIP

Not bad, huh? The guys out in the bullpen were no slackers, either:

Don Mossi 6–1, 1.94 ERA, 1.022 WHIP, 7 saves
Ray Narleski 3–3, 2.22 ERA, 1.157 WHIP, 13 saves
Hal Newhouser 7–2, 2.51 ERA, 1.14 WHIP

Overall, the 1954 Indians finished first in ERA (2.78), complete games (77), fewest hits allowed (1220), fewest runs allowed (504), and fewest walks allowed (486). They could get the strikeout when they needed it, too, ranking third in whiffs (678).

Also, the Tribe had an airtight defense backing-up their stellar pitching staff. Catcher Mike Hegan (.994), outfielder Larry Doby (.995), and infielder Bobby Avilla (.976) all finished first at their positions in fielding percentage. As a team, they posted a .974 percentage, good for second place in the American League.

The statistics clearly show that the 1954 Cleveland Indians were a very, very, VERY good team. With top-quality hitting, excellent pitching, and sure-handed fielders, a World Championship seemed likely. The Giants were a first-rate club, but the Indians had played like few teams ever have.

The "Jints" (as hometown fans sometimes referred to them) were resting much of their hopes on their pitching staff. It may not have been quite as good as Cleveland's during the regular season, but it was still high quality. Here's how Manager Leo Durocher's starting rotation performed in 1954:

Johnny Antonelli 21–7, 2.30 ERA, 1.171 WHIP
Ruben Gomez 17–9, 2.88 ERA, 1.403 WHIP
Sal Maglie 14–6, 3.26 ERA, 1.337 WHIP
Don Liddle 9–4, 3.06 ERA, 1.224 WHIP

In a short series, with days off for travel, Leo could use his top two guys twice, which would mitigate any advantage the Indians might have had in the comparison of starting rotations. If the starter got into trouble, Leo had some effective tools at his disposable out in the bullpen:

Hoyt Wilhelm 12–4, 2.10 ERA, 1.159 WHIP, 7 saves
Marv Grissom 10–4, 2.35 ERA, 1.226 WHIP, 17 saves
Windy McCall 2–5, 3.25 ERA, 1.295 WHIP, 2 saves

The National Leaguers finished first overall in ERA (3.09), fewest hits allowed (1258), fewest earned runs allowed (550), and shutouts (17). So, the Giants could pitch a little, too.

At the plate, New York was led by eventual NL MVP Willie Mays (.345 AVG, .411 OBP, 41 HRs, 110 RBIs). Backing-up the "Say Hey Kid" were outfielders Don Mueller (.342 AVG), Dusty

Rhodes (.341 AVG), and shortstop Al Dark (.293 AVG). Also, third baseman Hank Thompson drilled 26 home runs, and outfielder Monte Irvin tallied 19 homers.

The Giants ranked a respectable fifth in the NL in overall fielding percentage (.975), so they weren't killing themselves with the glove. Willie Mays played particularly well in the field, ranking second in percentage (.985), putouts (448), and range factor (3.08). Possessor of a rifle arm, Mays was number one in double plays turned by a centerfielder (9).

I do agree with most experts at the time who thought that Cleveland had the better team going into the World Series. But I don't see them as being *a lot* better. I base this largely on what I see as an edge in overall pitching (lower era, hits allowed, and earned runs allowed). Historically, good pitching has often been a deciding factor in the World Series. Notable examples include (but not limited to) the Fall Classics of 1963, 1967, 1968, 1974, 1985, 1991, and 2014.

The Tribe was a slightly better fielding team (.979 to .975). Offensively, the Giants had a small advantage. New York smashed more home runs (186 to 156) and hit for a marginally higher average (.264 to .262), but the Indians had a higher on-base percentage (.341 to .332) and scored more runs (746 to 732). Durocher's minions bettered the Indians in slugging (.424 to .403).

Something that few were paying attention to at the time was the fact that Indians racked-up many of their wins against teams in the AL that finished below .500 (89) and played just .500 against the second and third place clubs (Yankees and White Sox). Conversely, the Giants compiled a winning record (25–19) against their two closest competitors (Dodgers and Braves). Cleveland got "fat and sassy" feasting on their league's also-rans while the Giants were proving their mettle by doing well against their league's best. Had more of the experts thought about Cleveland's so-so record versus the AL elite, they might not have been so quick to believe that the Indians were going to roll over what they thought was an over-matched Giants club.

The 1954 World Series opened on September 29 at New York's home park, the Polo Grounds. Before almost 53,000 fans, the Giants began their march to the World Championship by topping the Indians 5–2 in ten innings. A sign that things that the fates may have been against the Tribe occurred in the 8th inning when Willie Mays made his now-famous spectacular catch of Vic Wertz's monster shot to centerfield. After snagging the ball, over the shoulder, Mays twirled around and fired an excellent throw to the infield that prevented the two runners that were on base from advancing. Had Number 24 missed the catch, a couple of runs would have scored, enabling the Indians to win the game.

Later, pinch-hitter Dusty Rhodes stroked a three-run, walk-off home run in the 10th inning to give the Giants the victory. Hardly a titanic blast, the ball barely made into the first few rows of seats just inside the right-field foul pole, a mere 296 feet from home plate. Losing pitcher Bob Lemon was so frustrated at being victimized by such a rinky-dink shot that he tossed his glove in disgust.

It looked like things were going to go better for the Indians in Game Two when Al Smith led-off with a home run. But starter Johnny Antonelli and reliever Don Mossi combined to keep Cleveland off the scoreboard for the rest of the game while Dusty Rhodes was making a major nuisance of himself again. The utility man from Alabama knocked-in two and hit another homer as the Giants went two-up with a 3–1 win.

Game three switched to Cleveland Stadium, but "home cooking" did nothing to reverse the Indians' fortunes. Once again, the pesky Rhodes was a key part of another Giant victory. His two-run, bases-loaded single in the third extended a New York lead to 4–0. Slugger Vic Wertz crashed a home run for the Indians, but it was one of just four hits his team would manage in a 6–2 loss.

On October 2, the Giants clinched it with a 7–4 win in front of over 78,000 disappointed Cleveland faithful. Dusty Rhodes sat this one out; the hitting stars for New York that day were Al Dark and Don Mueller (three hits each). A ton of head-scratching was going on by the experts who had been so sure the Indians would be the ones taking home the World Championship, not the upstarts from New York. But it shouldn't have been such a surprise for the reasons I shared earlier.

So why didn't the Indians win at least a game or two? Besides the obvious answer that the Giant outscored them in four different contests, that's almost impossible to answer with certainty. However, allow me to offer a couple of possibilities:

- Hubris. After winning 111 games with great hitting and a pitching staff that ranks among the all-time best, they may have thought they'd easily roll over the denizens of the Polo Grounds.
- A simple slump at the absolute worst time it could happen. The Indians had exactly one extended slump during the regular season, experiencing a four-game skid in July. As good as they were in 1954, they may have been due for another dry spell.

If I was forced to choose, I'd pick #2 as the most likely explanation. But I also think a degree of cockiness might have played a role in Cleveland's demise. There are almost assuredly other possibilities not discussed here. However, one thing is sure about the 1954 World Series:

A talented New York Giants club bested a fine Indians team to win it all.

1954 was a break-out season for Willie Mays (.345 AVG, 41 HR, 110 RBI). (Manny's Baseball Land via tradingcarddb.com)

Outfielder Dusty Rhodes was "Mr. Clutch" during the 1954 World Series. (Union Oil via tradingcarddb.com)

With hurlers like Hall-of-Famer Bob Feller in their rotation, the Indians looked like a sure bet to win the 1954 World Series. (1953 Bowman Gum trading card)

Larry Doby patrolled centerfield, drove in 126 runs and launched 32 homeruns for the American League pennant winners. (Bowman Gum)

Right-hander Sal "The Barber" Maglie contributed 14 wins to New York's 1954 pennant drive. (Jay Publishing via tradingcarddb.com)

Everything went right for Giants Manager Leo Durocher in the 1954 Fall Classic. (Baseball Digest)

CHAPTER 13

Nearly Identical (sort of)

Time to board the crazy train again. Earlier, I speculated about how the last-place 1973 Phillies might have won their division that year. And now this . . . what kind of season do you think a team would have with a starting line-up with batting stats that looked like this:

OF .306 AVG, .424 OBP, 7 HRs
OF .266 AVG, .329 OBP, 34 HRs
OF .245 AVG, .338 OBP, 13 HRs
3B .275 AVG, .330 OBP, 11 HRs
SS .236 AVG, .368 OBP
2B .260 AVG, .338 OBP, 11 HRs
1B .244 AVG, .306 OBP, 16 HRs
C   .241 AVG, .335 OBP

Also seeing playing time was a guy who hit .274 with a good .353 OBP, a seasoned veteran that ripped nine home runs in 142 plate appearances, and a multi-position utility man who registered an OK .248 batting average.

This fondly remembered team finished first in the league in walks (616), sixth in home runs (139), and fifth in triples (40). And finally, they were skippered by one of baseball's legendary, Hall-of-Fame managers.

If you had to make a guess based on the hitting stats, how many games do you think they won? Had I not done the research for this article, I would have estimated in the 55–65-win range. I'll give you a hint—this club took the field during one of the two eras when batting averages were historically low (1901 to 1919 or 1962 to 1969).

Next, let's examine the offensive performance of another famous team from the same era (it wasn't the same exact year). First the starting line-up:

OF	.259 AVG,	.315 OBP,	12 HRs
OF	.238 AVG,	.263 OBP,	10 HRs
OF	.274 AVG,	.361 OBP,	9 HRs
3B	.280 AVG,	.374 OBP	
2B	.250 AVG,	.337 OBP,	12 HRs
SS	.286 AVG,	.330 OBP	
1B	.238 AVG,	.334 OBP,	8 HRs
C	.233 AVG,	.289 OBP,	8 HRs

The reserves were no help at all in generating runs. The "most" productive part-timer posted a less-than-impressive line of .240 AVG, .290 OBP, and 3 home runs in 162 plate appearances. None of the other reserves hit more than one homer. The bench player with the most plate appearances (216) also had a low on-base percentage (.313), and only seven extra-base hits. The next three most-used subs put up averages ranging from .171 to .210 and OBP numbers from .243 to .304.

This club did finish first (out of ten teams) in stolen bases (172) and hit-by-pitches (52). However, they ended the season last in home runs (78), ninth in total bases (1820), eighth in runs (608), doubles (193), and triples (32). Also, this squad placed next-to-last in slugging percentage (.335). They, too, were skippered by a future Hall-of-Fame manager.

When compared with the first team's numbers, they had a higher overall batting average (.245 to .240) and hit more doubles (193 to 166). But they were out-homered (139 to 78), outscored (617–608), out-slugged (.361–.335), and the first club hit more triples (40–32) and drew more walks (616 to 492).

Based on these statistics, I might have guessed that the first team and second team finished with similar, albeit mediocre, records. Neither team looked like it had much "pop" in their line-up. They were probably second-division clubs, finishing at or near the bottom of the standings.

Sounds reasonable (at least to me).

Reasonable but *wrong*.

The first team was the 1962 New York Mets. With Hall-of-Fame manager Casey Stengel at the helm, they posted a historically dreadful record of 40 wins and 120 losses. Over the years, their first season on-field ineptitude plus a heaping portion of zaniness has made the newly minted Mets the stuff of legends. Many consider them the worst team of all-time. I don't agree with that assessment; there have been worse teams (1917 A's, 1935 Braves, 1942 Phillies, 1952 Pirates, and a few others). But the Mets were *bad*. Yeah, they had a few guys that got on base, but their pitching staff was *very bad*.

Atrocious would be a more accurate word to describe Casey's mound staff in 1962. I'm going to omit names to not further embarrass the legacy of those involved. Overall, the Mets finished last in ERA (5.04), hits allowed (1577), runs allowed (948), home runs surrendered (192), and strikeouts (772).

And their defense was awful, leading the league in errors while finishing dead last in fielding percentage. Considering their so-so offensive attack, brutal pitching, and a lousy defense, it's a wonder that the Mets won *any* games in 1962.

That second team, the one that posted worse overall batting stats than the 1962 Mets, was the 1965 World Champion Los Angeles Dodgers.

Whoa! How did they win 97 games with that squirt-gun offense?

For starters, with *great* pitching. Their rotation included Hall-of-Famers Sandy Koufax and Don Drysdale plus proven winners Claude Osteen and Johnny Podres. Together, that quartet won 71 and lost 41. The bullpen featured one of the league's best closers, Ron Perranoski, and the effective, reliable arms of veterans Jim Brewer, Howie Reed, and Bob Miller. With earned-run averages ranging from 1.82 to 3.12, these four collectively saved 31 games.

The 1965 Dodgers finished first in the league in ERA (2.81), complete games (58), shutouts (17), hits allowed (1223), and runs allowed (521). They were second in strikeouts (1079) and third in least bases-on-balls issued (425). Manager Walter Alston's pitchers ranked a relatively high fifth in home runs allowed (127), but that wasn't enough to negate all the other good things they were doing on the mound.

With the glove, the Boys from L.A. were no slouches, finishing second in team fielding percentage and third in the fewest number of errors committed. With incredible pitching and an excellent defense, the Dodgers didn't need to score a whole of runs. They scored an average of 3.70 runs-per-game (608 runs divided by 162 games) and allowed 3.08 runs-per-game (521 runs divided by 162 games), which means they won a lot of close ball games that season. And led by speedster Maury Wills' 94 steals, the denizens of Chavez Ravine were able to manufacture more-than-few runs without a ton of extra-base hits. A win is a win, whether it's by 10 runs or just one, and the Dodgers racked-up 97 of them in 1965 with what they had.

So, the 1965 Dodgers were a better team than the 1962 Mets. Not much of a revelation, is it? Talk about stating the obvious! But the 1962 Mets were fascinating, with a line-up that featured a handful of decent players with not-bad stats (Frank Thomas, Richie Ashburn, Felix Mantilla, Gil Hodges, Gene Woodling, and Jim Hickman). I think with, let's say average pitching, they could have approached the 70-win range and subsequently avoided the infamy of being one of the worst teams of all-time. What if they had been blessed with a pitching staff like the 1965 Dodgers? Well, they certainly wouldn't have lost 120 games! I think .500 plus would have been a real possibility. A contender? Almost assuredly not with that porous defense.

But the 1962 Mets weren't really about statistics, were they? As a collective unit, they embodied a spirit of good-natured fun that seems to be almost completely missing from today's professional game. Baseball would be a bit more enjoyable if every-now-and-then zany characters and teams like Stengel's crew in 1962 would appear to give us a laugh or two.

I'm glad they didn't have better pitching and defense.

Had they won a few more games, we would have been robbed of the enjoyable diversion that was the entertaining and madcap 1962 New York Mets.

Frank Thomas slammed 34 homeruns to pace a not-so-bad Mets hitting attack in 1962. (Jay Publishing via tradingcarddb. com)

Fireballer Sandy Koufax. No pitcher on the Mets could even carry this guy's rosin bag. (USC Libraries & California Historical Society)

Fan-favorite Marv Throneberry hit 16 homers for the Mets. (Jay Publishing via tradingcarddb.com)

Former Yankee star Gene Woodling wrapped-up his fine 17-year career by hitting .274 for the '62 Mets. (Bowman Gum)

Shortstop Maury Wills scored 92 runs and swiped 94 bases for the 1965 Dodgers. (Manny's Baseball Land via tradingcarddb.com)

CHAPTER 14

Visit to an Old Friend

The late summer morning had begun gray and had evolved lazily into a gloomy afternoon. On the train rumbling toward North Philadelphia, I passed the time apprehensively, looking up at the sky through the tinted rail window. The horizon was swollen and dark. Unlike some of my friends, I couldn't afford to waste money on train fare just to find out the game had been canceled. So, I hoped, prayed and crossed my fingers that the Phillies would play the Houston Astros as scheduled.

I grew up in the 1960s and 70s in that famous suburb northeast of Philly, Levittown, PA. We played a lot of sports in my neighborhood; with the Baby Boom in full swing, it was never hard to find enough kids to get a game to get a pick-up game of *something* going. And every now and then, a bunch of us would hop a train to Philly to see the Phillies play baseball at Connie Mack Stadium. The Phillies back then were terrible, but it was still fun to take the

45-minute train ride to see the big boys play ball. Plus, my pals and I always had a lot of laughs, even if the game stunk.

By the time of my last visit in August 1970, Connie Mack Stadium had deteriorated in proportion to the Phillies chronic lack of success on the field. The ballpark, built in 1909, was basically a dump. I remember ancient, filthy bathrooms that smelled awful and mildew that clung to the walls under the grandstand. Seating was bad; spectators paid for a couple of hours in hard, wooden chairs that had been painted numerous times to mask their age. A thin, opaque grime had settled on the ballpark, a gift courtesy of the smokestack industries that surrounded the neighborhood and the city.

Despite this, Connie Mack Stadium possessed certain charms, such as a neatly manicured, lush green grass playing surface. Beyond the stinky restrooms, your sense of smell was massaged by the aroma of hot dogs, popcorn, and beer. And if you weren't saddled with a seat obstructed by a metal support beam, it was a great place to watch a game. Fans were close to the action, and you didn't need binoculars to see the players.

I remember the air being oppressively heavy and moist that afternoon in August as my friends and I walked the six blocks from the train station to Connie Mack Stadium.

They'll NEVER play, I thought.

But I began to feel encouraged when the ballpark's prominent arc light standards became visible above the skyline. With each step, Connie Mack Stadium grew larger and larger and soon seemed bigger than anything nature could hurl its way.

Traffic around the ballpark was light, a harbinger of the eventual sparse crowd of less-than-4,000. The stadium's capacity was 33,000; few would have wanted to spend the afternoon in the sunshine watching the Phillies muddle their way through another hapless nine-innings, even less in what looked like an approaching rainstorm.

Lines at the ticket windows were nonexistent. My friends and I purchased our one-dollar admission tickets, bought programs for 50 cents that included a free, small red pencil to keep score with and headed for the dugout areas. Our seats were in the upper deck "nosebleed" section, but we wanted to get a few autographs before the game started. In those days, it was easier to do. There was less of a preoccupation with keeping fans away from the players.

The first player we pestered was Jesus Alou of the Astros. He was good-natured, talkative, and seemed to appreciate the attention.

"What is this?" he asked when my friend, Tim Holmes, handed him a program to sign. Alou pointed towards a photo of All-Star Mets pitcher Tom Seaver featured prominently on the front.

"How come no Phillies on the cover?" Alou asked. "They have some good players, no?"

"*No,*" someone, I forget who, wisecracked. Alou smiled as we snickered and scribbled his signature with one of those little red pencils across Tom Seaver's face.

Alou looked at me and said, "Maybe *you* be on this cover someday, no?"

The Houston outfielder was a large, muscular man, and being so close to him was a little intimidating. I smiled nervously and handed him my program. Alou quickly signed his name and reached for another souvenir.

A few minutes later, we migrated to the lower deck seating area near the left-field foul pole. Several Phillies were running wind sprints in the outfield. Grizzled veteran Jim Bunning seemed to be working the hardest.

As Bunning stopped momentarily to catch his breath, I leaned up against the rusty, metal screen and hollered, "Hey Jim! Do you think you'd have a better record if you pitched for a better team?"

Hands on his knees, Bunning looked up at me and looked like he was thinking.

"Son, I can't answer that," he finally said and then took off toward centerfield.

"He's washed-up," another one of my pals, Brian O'Donnell said.

Lee Burris, nicknamed "Fatman," shouted "Old geezer!" loud enough for everyone in the ballpark to hear.

Of all the guys-in-the-neighborhood, Lee was the one you could count on to say or do something outrageous.

"You better watch it, Fatman," Bobby Crouch warned. "He might come back and kick your butt."

Bobby was the leader of our pack, a smart kid with tons of athletic ability. He was a year older than me (I was 13 at the time); if Bobby had had a bent towards crime, we would have all probably ended up in jail. Instead, we kept ourselves busy much of the time playing sports.

Lee stuck out his chin, straightened his shoulders and clenched a fist.

"I'll kick *HIS* butt!" he announced.

The rest of us hooted, and Bobby said, "Yeah, right!"

Reserve infielder and pinch hitter Rick Joseph stretched his bulky sinews near the third-base coaching box. With a bead of perspiration rolling down his cheek, he glanced at the clouds that loitered over the stadium and muttered, "C'mon thundershower!"

Bobby and I watched him for a few moments, and then Bobby whispered, "What a lazy *bum*."

Joseph was a little bit too close for my friend to express himself any louder. I agreed with the analysis and nodded.

Just then, mountainous Houston first baseman John Mayberry walked by. He dwarfed my buddies and me, and if the sun had been out, it seemed like he could have cast a shadow on half of the lower deck.

We waited until it was almost game time to go to our seats. On the way up, all of us except Lee bought sodas; he bought a plastic cup of vanilla ice cream.

A few rows down, an old man in a battered Phillies cap champed on a fat cigar.

"This ice cream *sucks*," Lee announced.

"Like you," Tim Holmes several seats away and out of Ollie's beefy reach.

"Ooooooooooooooo!" went the rest of us.

Ollie flipped him the bird and then stood-up. At first, I thought he was going to take a poke at Tim. Instead, the Fatman walked down to the edge of the upper deck.

"You guys dare me to throw this at Joseph?" he asked.

"You better not," cautious Jerry Moore warned. "We might get in trouble."

"Shut-up, Spigot," Brian O'Donnell hissed. ("Spigot" was Jerry's nickname.)

"Yeah," I added. "Stop being a wienie!"

Jerry responded with rolled eyes and a shake of the head.

"You won't do it," Bobby told Lee.

"Wanna bet?"

"You're a wuss, you won't do it."

"Oh, yeah? Get down here, and you'll *see*."

Everyone, except Jerry, scrambled down several rows to join Lee.

"OK, there he is," Tim said, pointing at the target who was standing near the Phillies dugout.

With a mighty wind-up, Lee gave the partially eaten ice cream cup a pitch. The frozen novelty whizzed over the shoulder of an usher and landed—plop—smack-dab-on-top of the infielder's head.

"Nice shot, Sonny," the old fellow with the cigar said through clenched teeth.

It took Joseph a couple of seconds to realize what happened. When the partially melted ice cream began to ooze into his eyes, the infielder began to stomp around, wiping his face with his sleeves and saying things very loudly in Spanish.

After regaining his composure, Joseph looked up menacingly in our direction. All he saw were rows and rows of empty seats, an old guy with a beat-up Phillies cap, and five young choir boys, sitting innocently in anticipation of an afternoon of baseball.

We waited until Joseph stepped into the Phillies dugout, and then we laughed and laughed.

Even Jerry

The rain held off, and the game was played in its entirety. The sun even made several brief appearances, each time casting a sickly yellow glow over the playing field. Surprisingly, the Phillies won 4–0, thanks to good pitching by Rick Wise and a long home run by Deron Johnson. Whoopee! It wasn't exactly the seventh game of the World Series, but back then, Phillies fans took everything they could get.

From our perch along the first-base line, I remember feeling a gnawing sadness as I gazed around the nearly empty ballpark several times. The Phillies were scheduled to move into a shiny, new stadium in 1971. On one level, I looked forward to the change. A new ballpark would be cool, I thought. But as the game progressed, one thought dampened any enjoyment I might have experienced at the rare occurrence of a Phillies victory:

I was losing a *friend*.

Sure, Connie Mack Stadium was stinky and decrepit. But it had been a part of my life, all my life.

Soon, it would be gone.

Forever.

If my pals hadn't been around, I might have cried.

After the game, as we headed back to the train station for the trip home, I turned around slowly in the parking lot and took one long, last look at the old ballyard.

Large raindrops began to fall around us. A low rumble of thunder followed a moment later.

"We better roll, or we'll get soaked!" Bobby exclaimed.

With a sigh, I joined my pals as we began to run for the train.

Connie Mack Stadium. Gone but not forgotten! (Flickr by xnedski at https://www.flickr.com/photos/24358389@N00/2605290141)

Deron Johnson hit a long home run at old Connie Mack Stadium in August 1970. (1972 photo from Tickertron via tradingcarddb.com)

It was at this approximate spot in the upper deck that we watched the game in August 1970. (Nathan Hughes (Hamilton/https://creativecommons.org/licenses/by/2.0 /deed.en)

By 1970, Jesus Alou had been traded to
Houston. He was very friendly to us and
gladly gave autographs. (Jay Publishing
via tradingcarddb.com)

The Phillies moved across town to brand new, spacious Veteran's Stadium in 1971.
(Squelle/ https://creativecommons.org/licenses/by/2.0/deed.en)

Bibliography

BOOKS

Breslin, Jimmy, *Can't Anybody Here Play This Game?* (Chicago, IL: Irving R. Dean Publishing, 2002 edition)

Cohen, Richard and Neft, David, *The Sports Encyclopedia Baseball: 2004*, (St. Martins Griffin, New York, NY, 2004)

Honig, Donald, *The Philadelphia Phillies*, (New York, NY: Simon and Shuster, 1991)

James, Bill, *The New Bill James Historical Abstract*, (New York, NY: Free Press, 2003)

Kashhatus, William C., *September Swoon*, (University Park, PA: Keystone Books, 2004)

Pepper, Al, *Mendoza's Heroes: Fifty Batters Below .200*, (Punxsutawney, PA: Pocol Press, 2002)

Prebenna, David, *The Baseball Encyclopedia*, (New York, NY: Simon and Shuster, 1996)

Ritter, Lawrence S., *The Glory of Their Times*, (New York, NY: Harper Perennial Modern Classics, 2010 edition)

Westcott and Bilovsky, *The New Phillies Encyclopedia*, (Philadelphia, PA: Temple University Press, 1993)

WEBSITES

HTTP: sabr.org (Baseball's Forgotten Era: the 80s by Dan D'Adonna plus site information on Germany Schaefer, Wally Pipp, and Bill Nowlin)

www.baseballreference.com (numerous player, team and seasonal pages examined for statistics and other information)

www.baseball-almanac.com (numerous player, team and seasonal
 pages examined for statistics and other information)
www.deadballera.com/BeerDrinkersGermanySchaefer.html
www.yahoomovies.com
www.imdb.com
www.rottentomatoes.com
www.si.com/vault/1987/06/29/115643/just-a-pipp-of-a-legend
 (Just a Pipp of a Legend by Bruce Anderson)
www.snopes.com/sports/baseball/wallypipp.asp (Wally Pipp's
 Career-Ending Headache by David Mikkelson)
www.baseballfans.biz/issues-facing-major-league-baseball.html
www.multpl.com (U.S. population statistics)
www.baseballsgreatestsacrifice.com
http://m.mlb.com/new/article/180898342/baseball-players-who-
 died-in-war/ (Major League Stars Who Earned Their Stripes
 by Lindsay Berra)
www.baseballinwartime.com
http://deadspin.com/5820716/the-100-worst-baseball-players-of-
 all-time-a-celebration-part-1 (The 100 Worst Players of All
 Time: A Celebration, Part 1 by Eric Nusbaum)
www.thenewamerican.com/culture/biography/
 item/10976-remembering-the-amazing-mets-of-1962
http://metsdaddy.com

About the Author

CHRIS WILLIAMS is a veteran freelance writer with numerous books, articles, and features to his credit. He is also a regular contributor to the Baseball Almanac Website and a member of the Central PA chapter of the Society for American Baseball Research. Chris loves dogs and when he's not hunched over a computer working on a manuscript, he's employed as a certified Pet Trainer at a local pet store. Chris and his wife Sue have lived in York County, PA since the early 1990s.